Safe Home Visits

By Chris Puls

© Copyright 2006 Chris Puls.

All rights reserved. No part of this publication may be reproduced, stored in a retrieval system, or transmitted, in any form or by any means, electronic, mechanical, photocopying, recording, or otherwise, without the written prior permission of the author.

Note for Librarians: A cataloguing record for this book is available from Library and Archives Canada at www.collectionscanada.ca/amicus/index-e.html
ISBN 1-4120-9292-2

Printed in Victoria, BC, Canada. Printed on paper with minimum 30% recycled fibre. Trafford's print shop runs on "green energy" from solar, wind and other environmentally-friendly power sources.

TRAFFORD

Offices in Canada, USA, Ireland and UK

Book sales for North America and international:
Trafford Publishing, 6E–2333 Government St.,
Victoria, BC V8T 4P4 CANADA
phone 250 383 6864 (toll-free 1 888 232 4444)
fax 250 383 6804; email to orders@trafford.com

Book sales in Europe:
Trafford Publishing (UK) Limited, 9 Park End Street, 2nd Floor
Oxford, UK OX1 1HH UNITED KINGDOM
phone +44 (0)1865 722 113 (local rate 0845 230 9601)
facsimile +44 (0)1865 722 868; info.uk@trafford.com

Order online at:
trafford.com/06-1046

10 9 8 7 6 5 4 3 2

Special Thanks:

It would be impossible to list all the people who have helped me gain the knowledge that I have shared within this book. This does not make my gratitude to them any less. However, there are people I would like to mention in particular. I would like to express special thanks to my parents who gave me far more guidance and support than I realized till much later in my life. To my husband, Mike, who has supported me both emotionally and financially many times during our life together. To the men and women in blue that I worked with and who taught me to be safe on the street. To Sensei Swart, thank-you for getting me started in the martial arts. To all my Sensei's- you have taught me more than I may ever know. To all my friends that have given me help, support and encouragement, not only for this book, but also in many different aspects of my life. To those above and to those that space just wouldn't allow- Thank you all.

INDEX

Prologue - pg. 9

Attention Employers - pg. 11

Personal safety can be frightening - pg. 15

"It won't happen to me" syndrome - pg. 17
    Examples of real crimes
    Statistics

S.A.T. Self-assessment - **Pg.** 21

Jane's story - pg. 27

Knowledge is your best weapon - pg. 33
    Why physical defense tips are not in this book
    Practice is critical

Denial is your enemy - pg. 39
    Rationalization
    Justification
    Minimization
    Excuse Making
    Refusal

What do predators want? - pg. 43
    Easy targets defined and described

What are predators relying on? - pg. 45
    Ignorance
    Fear response

Understanding the effects of fear - pg. 47
   How your body can work against you

Overcoming Fear - pg. 51
   The movie method
   My encounter with "Frank"
   Speaking of vocalizations...
   Throwing the criminals off guard

Do you look like a victim? – pg. 63
   Confident body language
   How you speak

Trust your instincts - pg. 71
   The many forms of intuition
   Stranger or strangeness?
   Real or Imagined?

Awareness is critical! – pg. 77
   Subtle clues

Warning signals - pg. 81
   Out of the ordinary
   "He was so nice"
   The power of "We"
   Compelling Statements
   "I promise"
   T.M.I.
   "No"
   Body Positioning
   "Body Language"
   Tone of voice
   Fights in the household
   About the warning signals

False indicators - pg. 105
    Mental Conditions
    Antisocial Personality Disorder
    ADHD
    Bi-Polar Disorder
    Schizophrenia
    Tourette's Syndrome
    Learning Disabilities
    Cultural Differences
    Personal space
    Physical contact
    Eye contact
    Women in business
    Non-verbal signals

The "What If's" - pg. 111
1. Client drunk or on drugs
2. Controlling client
3. Inappropriately dressed client
    - Claims of rape
4. First call makes you uncomfortable
    - Verify client info
    - Keep info safe
    - Take a friend
5. Not comfortable with client location
6. You find weapons or illegal items
7. Fight erupts between client and third party
8. Client not taking needed meds
9. Verbally abusive/threatening client
    - Types of threats
10. Third person makes you uncomfortable
11. Uncontrolled pets
    - Loose dog encounters
12. Excessive distractions
13. No spouse present- Jealousy possible

14. Medical Emergency
15. Client insists on your help
16. Called to help third party
17. Client blocks the exits
    Follow don't lead
    Client locks the door
18. Hazardous or appalling living conditions
19. You witness a crime
20. Client shows you a weapon
About the situations

How to get out - pg. 147
You don't have to stay
Cell Phones
Have a Signal
Know the address
Keeping Track- info for your lifeline
The excuses

Plans/preparations (over 55 safety tips) - pg. 157
Safety in numbers
Violent visitors
Auto related safety
Clothing
Food and drinks
Leave your stuff
General tips

Abduction Avoidance – Pg. 181

About rape – pg. 187

Weapons- yes or no - pg. 189
Guns
Chemical Spray

Pepper Spray
　　　Stun Gun
　　　Tazer
　　　Self Defense

Other situations - pg. 197
　　　Fire
　　　Medical Emergencies
　　　Unsafe or unsanitary living conditions

Insurance - pg. 201

Places you can get more information - pg. 203

Aftermath - pg. 205
　　　Effects of traumatic stress
　　　What to do after an attack

My wish to you - pg. 211

Notes about the S.A.T. assessment – pg. 215

Recommended Books and Videos - pg. 219

Prologue

I chose to write this book because personal safety is a topic near and dear to my heart. I also enjoy helping others learn how to be as safe as possible. Over the years, I have helped many people think about the dangerous possibilities as well as the solutions to get them out safely.

I started training in the martial arts when I was a young teen and it taught me many valuable lessons that I have carried with me as I moved from city to city and from one form of martial arts to another. It has given me a solid base from which to work in learning how to look at situations and how to read people.

As an adult, I went into the field of Law Enforcement and spent eight and a half years on patrol as a police officer in the City of Cincinnati. The things I saw and situations in which I found myself raised my personal safety awareness to new levels. It also increased my motivation to help others with personal safety concerns.

When I left the Law Enforcement field and went to work as a Professional Organizer, I found in talking with other organizers, that there are very few educational opportunities available to them about their safety during home visits. I did some research and found that although there are several professions that take people into other's homes, there was also very little information on personal safety available for most of these professionals. I knew I had the knowledge to change that and I went to work on this book. Now I travel the country teaching others in person about safety.

If you need a speaker, please consider me.
www.SafeHomeVisits.com

> My goal is to teach you to be more aware of things that you may not otherwise think about until it's too late. I will give you solutions and escapes to many uncomfortable situations in which you could find yourself.
>
> I will show you the benefits of having a plan of action.
>
> You do not need to have any martial arts training to implement the solutions in this book.

The solutions are written for anyone that enters the homes or personal spaces of persons they may be meeting for the first time or that they have known as clients or patients for a long time. But the information doesn't have to stop there. You will find that it carries over into your personal life as well, and that's an added benefit!

You will find that you are more aware of the warning signals given by others and by the development of certain situations without being paranoid about them.

You will gain a healthy awareness that can alert you to developing danger before it is too late to react, regardless of the situation, whether it be at work, while on a date, during a night on the town, whenever.

Attention Employers

The safety of your employees is your responsibility. The risk management supervisor should include important safety concerns in the policies and procedures manual so that everyone can be safe.

Make sure your company or organization has Risk Management policies in writing that handle 'in home' situations. These are written rules for how certain situations should be handled. Do those Risk Management procedures include the relevant items discussed in this book?

What would happen if one of your employees was seriously hurt or killed and the media ran the story on the six o'clock news? If you are in denial and believe that "It won't happen," please read the rest of this book for the facts.

Read the news clippings and statistics at the beginning of this book and realize that it only takes one mentally unbalanced person to completely change the life of the employee and the image of the company. It would be easier to institute and enforce certain security measures than to deal with the tragic aftermath of an incident.

> The courts have consistently held employers liable for protecting employees from known hazards and for the peace and efficiency in the workplace.[1]

This book covers several of the possible hazards that could be considered "known" even if you never read this book; Things that the courts could consider "a reasonable risk that you should have foreseen and taken measures to prevent". You may have better legal footing if policies are in place (and enforced) to protect your employees. However, policies and procedures will not hold any weight if most of the employees can say they were not aware of the risks and policies or that the policies were never used.

Preparation and education can greatly reduce a person's chances of becoming a victim of crime. If an employee does become a victim, chances are high that it will negatively affect their work performance (if they are able to continue to work.)

Some of these effects could include:
- Feeling angry and taking it out on others.
- Desire for revenge or vengeance.
- Replaying the event in the mind repeatedly is common. Their mind will not be on their work.
- Feeling afraid that the attacker will find them or that another attack will occur if they go back to work.
- Pervasive fear and/or anxiety.
- Self destructive or impulsive behaviors.
- Not being able to sleep or having terrible nightmares.
- Feeling helpless or ineffective because it seems control of their life has been lost.
- Not wanting to be left alone or to work alone
- Trouble concentrating and making decisions.
- Crying uncontrollably or a feeling of no emotions.
- Hyper sensitive to touch or sudden noises.
- Depression

For more information, a web search for "work place violence policies" can enlighten you. OSHA also has many pages on their website devoted to work place violence, its recognition and prevention. Go to: **www.osha-slc.gov** and type in "workplace Violence" in the site search box.

Another crime employers can help prevent is impaired driving. If you know that an employee is impaired due to medications or alcohol, you should not allow that person to drive. The courts have "grey" areas concerning employer liability for accidents or deaths caused by an employee that was known to be impaired. However, million dollar court fines are not the only risk. If the employee gets into an accident you could have loss of work from that person, increased health insurance claims and increased motor vehicle insurance (if they drive a company car). If they are arrested for being impaired, they will have time away from work for court appearances and possibly jail time. It is likely the person's driving license will be suspended. If the employee is killed it will affect his or her co-workers. This can cause reduced productivity during mourning. There may also be negative media coverage if the employee kills someone else and is found to be impaired. Impaired driving is very costly for business and being proactive to stop it can save large sums of business money.

If you would like me to speak to your employees, I am available to do seminars and workshops for your company, organization or group. Session length and content is flexible to meet your needs.

Seminars assure that employees are informed.

For more information about the presentations I offer, please visit my website: **www.SafeHomeVisits.com**
To inquire about my availability to do a seminar, please email me at **SafeHomeVisits@hotmail.com**

Personal safety can be frightening

Safety is not something most people think about on a regular basis. Some jobs, by their very nature, put people at higher risk of crime than others. If your job requires you to work alone and/or visit clients in their homes, you need to read this book.

Many home visitors have the feeling that "It won't happen to me" or "I don't work with that type of client". As uncomfortable as the thought may be, anyone could cause you harm. Just because that person lives in an affluent area, in a big beautiful home, it does not mean that person may not have a mental imbalance or drug problem or violent tendencies. There are also other dangers that don't necessarily involve a crime.

Some of the possible crimes that home visits could present include: robbery, theft, stalking, verbal abuse, sexual crimes or harassment, murder, and physical abuse or threats. Other issues and hazards that could arise include: ice, weapons, poor condition of the home, medical emergencies, dangerous animals and even fire.

My own surveys have shown that women think about their safety or have uncomfortable feelings about situations much more often than men. Because of this, my book is written primarily using a female visitor and a male client. This is not meant to imply that the information is not of use to men that want to feel safer or that only male clients can be dangerous.

When a person first starts thinking about her safety and all the horrible "what-if's" that could happen, she usually gets overwhelmed and stops thinking about it. It is much easier to say," It won't happen to me," "I'm careful" or "My job isn't dangerous."

The reason this happens is because the "What If's" don't provide any safe solutions.

> If you only think about what could happen and don't look at solutions, you are left feeling very vulnerable.

I encourage you to finish this book, even if you are made uncomfortable in the beginning. It is natural to want to get away from things that cause fear and we will later discuss how you can use that to your advantage.

Please brave the fear of reading about the situations presented in this book so that you can gain powerful knowledge that will help you conquer the paralyzing fear of a real situation.

"It won't happen to me" syndrome

When you know what to do to stay safe, you will be less afraid of the unknown. Part of learning to stay safe is to get rid of the "It won't happen to me" mentality. Having an awareness of the possibilities is good; denial that it could happen to you is not. There are far more crimes committed than are ever reported. The ones that are reported become statistics and those statistics are frightening. Don't rely on luck or "the odds"-- take a proactive roll in keeping yourself safe.

> I am not trying to frighten you; I'm trying to open your eyes to the possibilities so you can see that your safety should be considered.

Here are just a few examples of crimes that have already occurred:

- A 63-year-old real estate agent was raped at knifepoint inside a vacant Coral Gables home by a man who had an appointment to see the property.[2]

- A caseworker for a children's services agency was stabbed to death while interviewing a couple... She had been making regular visits with the family trying to unify them.[3]

- A nurse was killed after she discovered two victims shot by the son of her patient. The nurse was shot while making a call to 911. This took place in Girard, a town of about 4,000 people in southeast Kansas.[4]

- A 27-year-old social worker was at a family's apartment to discuss a case plan with the parents. The father was the only one home when the social worker arrived. She stayed and explained the case plan to him.

    As she prepared to leave, he grabbed her by the throat and pulled one of her arms behind her. He then took the woman into the dining room and showed her a suicide note he had written. He forced her into the living room and raped her on a mattress.[5]

- A Child Welfare worker is beaten with a hammer and suffocated during a home visit.[6]

- A Daytona Beach real estate agent was stabbed to death by someone apparently posing as a customer.[7]

- Two female real estate agents were showing an open house in an upscale neighborhood in Cincinnati Ohio when a man with a gun arrived. He forced them into the basement, removed their clothing and assaulted them for about 45 minutes before he robbed them and left. They said the man threatened kill them.[8]

Statistics:
In a study of the information from the U.S. Department of Labor- Bureau of Labor Statistics, it was found that between 1992 and 2002 there were 724 deaths of

workers in residences. This includes only victims that died from assaults and violent acts. This does not take into consideration the victims that survived an attack and all the attacks and attempts that went unreported.[9]

> Crimes happen to all types of people. You are not protected just because of your geographic area, the social status of the client, your race, your age or any other demographic.

The best protection is knowledge of how to recognize a potentially dangerous situation as it develops and knowing how to either diffuse the situation or get out of it quickly.

Protecting Yourself From Violence During Home Visits by Chris Puls

S.A.T. Self-assessment

S.A.T. in this case stands for:
- **S**tay aware
- **A**ct on the warning signals
- **T**rust your instincts

What is your S.A.T. score? Answer the following questions to find out. Then re-take the assessment after you have read through the book. There are not too many choices below that would be dangerous for you to do, but some choices would raise your chances of becoming a victim more than others.

Stay aware:

1. When you walk to the client's home, where are you looking?
    a. I watch the ground and pavement so I don't trip
    b. I'm looking at the house to check for possible warning signals
    c. I'm casually checking the area to all sides of me for possible danger
    d. All of the above

2. When I'm with a client
    a. I'm completely focused on them and their needs
    b. I'm focused on the needs of the client, but check occasionally on the surroundings
    c. I'm comfortably aware of all that is going on around me

3. If someone I just met was being extra kind, was telling me all about themselves, and was sure I could help them even when I wasn't sure
    a. I would work with them, they seem really nice
    b. I would not hesitate to leave and refuse to work With them
    c. I would look for more warning signals or trust my instincts

4. When I'm in public
    a. I keep to myself and don't make eye contact
    b. I'm always keeping watch of my surroundings; I could be a secret service agent
    c. I make casual eye contact with as many people as possible

5. I know that it takes a criminal about ___ seconds of observation to select his victim
    a. 30 seconds
    b. 15 seconds
    c. 2 - 7 seconds

6. I spot potential dangers in the home like letter openers, fire place pokers and kitchen knives.
    a. I don't let them concern me because I don't work with violent clients
    b. I make sure the client puts these away
    c. I remain aware of their location and use body positioning if needed to keep the client away from these items.

7. While driving to a client's home, you notice that the car that is behind you appears to be making all the same turns as you.

    a. I make some turns I didn't plan to make to see if he follows and I hope I don't get lost
    b. I don't go to the client's home but stay on streets I know varying my speed to see if he stays behind me.
    c. I pull into a busy parking lot and see if he follows me
    d. I would try b and/or c

Act on the signals:

8. When someone makes me uneasy or I just don't trust them:
    a. If I feel unsafe, I immediately break off contact with them and if necessary I have another colleague work with them, preferably a male.
    b. If I'm not feeling danger, I continue to work with them and dismiss the feelings.
    c. If I don't sense danger, I raise my awareness level and watch for any other warning signals
    d. I could do a or c

9. You have arrived at the home of a client you have been working with for quite awhile. However, he seems to be more edgy, he is fidgeting, jumpy and distracted. This is not the behavior you have come to expect from this usually level headed and calm client. What do you do?
    a. I end the session because he obviously can't concentrate
    b. I tell him I noticed his behavior and ask him if everything is OK
    c. I raise my awareness levels and watch for signs of danger
    d. I could do any of the above depending on the feelings I get about the situation.

10. You have been working with a client but it's not working out for reasons related to the work you were doing. You have gotten some minor warning signals from him in the past and he makes you uncomfortable. You tell him at the end of your last session that you won't be back and that you can't continue to work with him. He says he understands but then he says that you must not be competent enough to handle his needs. He says; "It's OK; I understand why you have to leave me helpless." How do you handle this?
   a. I feel sorry for him and offer to work with him for a few more sessions till he can find a replacement
   b. I feel the need to make the parting more amicable and stay to explain my reasons for leaving so he won't be upset.
   c. My intentions have been made clearly, I remain silent and leave

11. You have been working in the basement or second floor of the client's home. When you need to use the stairway, he blocks it from use. He's just joking around and has a big friendly smile on his face. You ask him politely to move but he doesn't. When you ask a second time, less politely, he moves and apologizes.
   a. I don't let the behavior bother me because he was just joking
   b. I explain that his behavior was completely inappropriate and made me very uncomfortable
   c. I walk directly out of the house, get a friend or co-worker on my cell phone and ask the client to deliver my belongings outside to me. I don't work with that client again.

12. When you sit down with a client, he sits much closer than is really necessary and it makes you uncomfortable.
    a. I don't want to be rude so I just work through it
    b. I move over a bit to give myself more room
    c. I ask him to please move over and give me some space

Trust your instincts

13. You are meeting with a male client that seems nice and says he will be alone. You have not gotten any warning signals from him so you are comfortable with that. However, when you arrive you find that some of his male friends have "stopped by for a visit." They are not giving you any of the warning signals.
    a. You leave immediately
    b. You politely ask him to have his friends leave
    c. Your awareness level is substantially raised and you are ready to leave at any moment if you feel uncomfortable
    d. I could do any of the above depending on how I felt about the situation

14. As you are talking with a client, you notice he is standing in a defensive stance like boxers use. His eye contact could be described as drilling into your eyes. His body seems relaxed and his tone is calm.
    a. He's probably a police officer I wouldn't let it bother me
    b. I would raise my awareness level to watch for signs that his attitude is getting more hostile.
    c. I would have him sit down to continue the conversation and watch for any signals that his attitude is getting more hostile.

15. Related to number 7 above (you think you are being followed in your car): Even after your maneuvers the person has stayed with you. What do you do?
    a. I would stay in a well populated place till he left
    b. I would call my office or a friend from my cell phone to report the man
    c. I would call the police and explain the situation, giving the license plate number, vehicle description and driver description if I was able to safely get that information. Then I would stay in a well populated location until the police arrived.

Now read on to see how you did. If this is your second time through the test, go to the back of the book for some discussion of the possible choices.

Jane's Story

The following story was chosen because it illustrates several key signals as well as showing an extreme possibility. *I will be referring back to it to point out the warning signs that were not recognized until it was too late. Keep in mind that this story does not give you the solutions, so it may be frightening.* You will need to continue reading to understand what Jane could have done to avoid being a victim.

It was on a beautiful spring day that "Jane" learned that she should have listened to her intuition. She was a successful realtor and it was about a week prior to the incident, that a nice looking man came to her office requesting her services to help him sell his home. He seemed nice enough, but she was immediately very uneasy with him. Looking back she now recognizes some of the reasons, but at the time all she had was her gut feeling, which she brushed aside.

During that first meeting she got all the standard information from her new client. He said his name was Greg and his home was located in a part of town known to be a very nice area. Jane's company policy required her to check the driver's license or identification of any new clients, but when she asked to see Greg's, he said it had been stolen while he was at work. He said he worked in a bad neighborhood and that it was a really nice leather wallet that his wife had given him. She thought to herself that the man was a victim of one of the most common crimes in the area, theft. She assumed that he hadn't yet had the chance to get a new I.D. card. She told him it wouldn't be a problem and verbally got the information she needed to fill out the new client forms.

As the paperwork was filled out, they carried on a casual conversation. He asked if she lived on his side of town and she told him that she worked in that area, but she lived on the other side of town. Greg asked how long she had been a realtor and she told him proudly "eleven years." He said, "You must have entered the profession right out of high school--you look so young." Jane thanked him and admitted that she was thirty-one.

He told her that the new house was in a great city and gave her some of the features of the new house that he really liked. He said that just like their old house, it was peaceful and secluded. Plenty of woods around and the neighbor's homes were hardly even visible. He said his wife was already working in the new city they were going to call home and that he was staying in the current home to give it a 'lived in' appearance. She noticed he wasn't wearing a ring but dismissed it as 'no big deal.' Lots of guys don't wear rings, right? Greg asked Jane if she was married; she said that she wasn't.

He told her, in great detail, about his kids including their ages, their grades, that they were honor students and all about their hobbies. It was obvious that he thought highly of them. He asked if she had any kids. She said she didn't but that she would really like to someday. She asked him if he had any pictures of his kids and he replied that they were already packed up. She thought she may have noticed a bit of hesitation in that answer, but thought it was probably embarrassment that he didn't have his children's pictures with him or that they were stolen along with his license.

At the conclusion of the meeting, they agreed to meet again at his home the following week. Aside from doing a check on the market value of homes in that area, Jane set his folder aside till the meeting. She sensed that something was not right but couldn't put a finger on it so again she dismissed the thought.

He seemed like a nice guy, married with children and living in a nice neighborhood. She had worked with lots of men fitting his description and nothing had ever been wrong in the past.

When she arrived at Greg's home, she was once again immediately unsettled but couldn't figure out the reason.

The home was very nice, even though the grass had not been cut. She noticed there were no curtains on the windows, but assumed that they were already packed. Greg greeted her with a charming smile as he met her at her car. He said, "Welcome to my home" and reached out to close her car door. As he did so, the folder she had under her arm was accidentally knocked to the ground.

He said, "I'm so sorry" as he picked it up and although she held out her hand, he ignored it and put his other hand on her elbow to direct her toward the house in front of him. That contact sent ice though her veins.

She felt herself pull away slightly and hesitate and he removed his hand. Her inner voice was saying "STOP, Something's wrong!" but she told herself to "stop worrying, you're over reacting."

He said "After you. We have a house to sell" and indicated the path up the walkway. She walked slightly ahead of him as she tried to focus on the job and point out to him how the yard could be spruced up. She stopped as she was talking to point out a hedge that needed trimming.

He told her "I have a yard service coming tomorrow so we don't need to worry about that hedge. I want to show you the inside of the house. You're going to love it, I promise."

At the front door, he reached in front of her to open it and put a hand gently on her back as she stepped though. She immediately noticed a total lack of any personal belongings. No furniture, no boxes, no sign that anyone lived there. By this time, her senses were screaming at her to RUN!

It was at that point he cupped a gloved hand around her mouth from behind, pulled her close and showed her the biggest knife she thought she had ever seen. She heard the door close behind them.

She was forced to the basement, bound and gagged then raped. When he was done, he whispered in her ear, "If you report me, I'll come to your apartment on Elm Street to kill you AND your room mate."
Then he left the house.

She felt a sense of relief when she heard the front door close and realized she had survived. The relief was mixed with the fear that he instilled when she realized he knew where she lived and that she had a roommate! She also had no idea how she would get out, but knew she couldn't just lie there.

She managed to get her bound feet under her and hop up the stairs to the front door. Once on the lawn, a woman walking her dog saw Jane and rushed to help her.

Greg was never caught and Jane lives in fear every day that he will find her and carry out his promise. She has moved and no longer works as a realtor.

> Greg was not caught because the house never belonged to him and all the information he initially gave to Jane was bogus. It is likely he will do this again.

The police couldn't even find prints because he wore gloves and apparently wiped the doorknob, her car door and the file folder. The house had been recently foreclosed and was not yet on the market so it didn't appear when Jane did the market analysis.

There were warning signs present from the very first contact. Many of them will be pointed out in subsequent chapters as I give you solutions you can use to prevent yourself from being caught in a situation like Jane's.

Knowledge is your best weapon

Knowledge is a very powerful weapon; Such as, knowing how to read people's intentions, how to avoid dangerous situations, how to get out of dangerous situations and what to do in an emergency. All of this knowledge is very empowering.

On the flip side is a lack of knowledge, no definite answers and fear of the unknown. These leave you vulnerable and can cause fear that is visible. Jane's unease during the first encounter was visible and Greg saw it.

Of all the possible strategies you might use to protect yourself, do you think worry and fear brought on by imagined risks are effective? No. Worry actually increases your risk because it interferes with the safety mechanism you are given naturally, your instincts. I'll teach you how to develop your instincts so you can have less worry and will only feel fear when it is warning you of valid and immediate danger. Worry is the fear we manufacture; it is a choice. True fear is involuntary; it will come and get your attention when necessary. If you always worry, you may not recognize the valid fear signals.

Denial is another threat to your safety. If you deny the possibility that something can happen, you blind yourself to the warning signals. You won't believe the signals you are seeing because you don't believe what they are warning you about could happen. I'll show you how to overcome denial.

> I will give you the empowering knowledge that could literally save your life and can help prevent you from becoming a Jane (or Jane Doe).

In a later chapter, I will give you some simple "escape lines" you can practice saying in case you find yourself in a bad situation.

Physical self defense moves are not covered here. There are plenty of books on that topic as well as places you can go to learn the techniques with the help of an instructor.

If you choose to expand on what I provide here by gaining physical defense knowledge, keep the following in mind; Physical defense knowledge is only good if you practice it regularly and correctly. If you take a self-defense course (something I encourage), please find friends or family that you can practice with on a regular basis. Not only will it help you, but it will help them as well if you take turns switching roles.

You need to build and maintain the "muscle memory" of the defensive actions to make them most effective and "second nature" to you. Practice the moves slowly at first while you work on perfecting the technique. As you become more proficient, your speed will automatically increase while maintaining the proper technique.

In the event of a confrontation, you don't have time to carefully analyze where you need to strike or grab, it should just happen. If you have not had extensive practice of self defense moves during adrenalin producing situations, you may not be able to fight your way free as effectively as you might think. Don't let a single self defense course give you a false sense of security. If you get into a physical confrontation, and find that you can not recall anything that you learned (a natural occurrence without extensive practice) then you might be setting yourself up for increased stress during the incident and increased mental trauma after the incident.

Don't get me wrong, I DO recommend that you learn to physically defend yourself. I just want to be sure you are going about it in an informed manner. Whether you learn one technique or master a whole repertoire of martial arts moves, proper practice is the key to making it effective.

Any physical skill requires some level of muscle memory training. Using a hammer, driving a car and dancing are all examples. Just as these skills get better and more fluid with practice, so does self defense.

Think back to when you first started driving. Were your stops smooth? Could you get the car moving again from a stop without it jerking or stalling? If the car had a standard transmission, how many times did the car stall or jerk?

Now think of your current driving skills. If you drive a lot then they have probably become second nature. You don't have to take time to think about making a smooth stop or start, it just happens.

Self defense can be just as complicated as the skills needed for driving. Often times it is even more difficult. Then add in the stress of a situation that would require the use of physical self defense and it should be clear why practice is so critical.

> Physical self defense skills can be considered most effective when the technique "just happens," without thought, as an automatic reaction to an attack.

When you choose a course or martial arts style, be sure it is effective in real life situations for women. Most classes and martial arts styles are designed to be effective for fights and bar room brawls. Crimes against women don't usually involve a fist fight. Men that attack women mostly use grabs, holds, pin down techniques and knocking the woman down. While they may also use their fist, it's not usually the first contact. Focus on courses that help you break out of holds and that teach you to fight from the ground. Aikido and Judo are examples of these styles.

If you choose just a few moves that work for you, once you are able to perform the techniques *correctly* and easily, find a friend or two that will help you practice and produce some adrenalin.

Have them do this by simulating an attack as realistically (but safely) as possible using speed and realistic verbal abuse. The first several times you will find that the moves that came easily will now be much harder to recall. Working through that natural effect will help you if you ever have a need for real-life use of the technique.

Please always practice safely with proper padding. You don't want to hurt your training partner and they should not be hurting you. I don't recommend "pulling" your punches, in other words, holding back some force. The reason is that if you practice by holding back, when it comes time for the real thing, you are more likely to hold back automatically because that is the muscle memory you have trained into your body. Instead, use professional padding for protection of the "aggressor" and to protect your hands, feet and face. This padding is available for sale at many martial arts dojo's (training centers) and some sporting goods stores.

The more you practice using the moves with adrenalin in your system the easier it will be to maintain your composure in a real situation.

In the next few sections, I'll teach you about overcoming automatic fear responses that interfere with thinking and movement. With some attacks, you may need to fake submission until you get an opening you can use. Once you get the opening don't hesitate-- explode with every ounce of your being and use any method you can to get free and get away.

> Mental and physical practice of the solutions listed in this book will help prepare you for the stress of a real life situation.

Many people feel they are not strong enough to physically protect themselves. This is a defeatist attitude. Think of someone you dearly love such as your kids, your spouse or your pet. Now imagine that someone is hurting them. Would you be able to use force to protect them? Many people say they could protect others that they love, but are unwilling to add their own name to the list of loved ones. Please add yourself to that list!

Truth is that if something happens to you it hurts the people you love. So defending yourself with the same level of force and determination you have reserved for others will also be protecting them.

Denial is your enemy

Imagine two dogs meeting on a sidewalk. One dog growls, shows his teeth, the hair over his shoulders goes up, his tail is raised like a flag, his ears are laid back. He crouches then attacks. It's not likely that the other dog is thinking "Gee, I never saw THAT coming!"

There were plenty of pre-attack signals that were given if the dog understood what to look for. He also needed to believe that the other dog was aggressive and that an attack was possible. Some dogs that have not had much contact with other dogs do not know how to read "dog language" and might misinterpret these pre-attack signals as play or not know what to think of them.

Many humans are the same way. They have not had the training or exposure to dangerous humans to have learned what the signals are. The signals can be just as obvious as the signals of the dog above once you know what to watch for. This book will help teach you about those signals.

Just because you don't know how to read these signals, does not mean that the violence they predict doesn't exist. Violent acts CAN be predicted. They don't happen "all of a sudden" or "out of the blue" unless you have missed the warning signals.

> Denial is CHOOSING to not know something.

The reason denial is your enemy is because it blinds you to the signals. If you deny that you could ever be attacked, you will talk yourself out of seeing the warning signals until they are so obvious that they can not be denied any longer.

All animals (humans included) are blessed with natural warning signals of danger. But humans are the only ones that routinely dismiss or try to explain away these warnings until it's too late. Instincts are discussed in more detail in another section. Suffice to say here, that if you are in denial, you are hindering your natural means of self preservation.

Signs of denial, with examples from Jane's story:

- Rationalization- "She thought to herself that the man was a victim of one of the most common crimes in the area, theft. She assumed that he hadn't yet had the chance to get a new I.D. card."
- Justification- "She thought she may have noticed a bit of hesitation in that answer, but thought it was probably embarrassment that he didn't have his children's pictures with him or that they were stolen along with his license."
- Minimization- "She noticed he wasn't wearing a ring but dismissed it as 'no big deal.' Lots of guys don't wear rings, right?"
- Excuse Making- "He seemed like a nice guy, married with children and living in a nice neighborhood. She had worked with lots of men fitting his description and nothing had ever been wrong in the past."

- <u>Refusal</u>- "She sensed that something was not right but couldn't put a finger on it so again she dismissed the thought."

Denial is common when it comes to facing dangerous possibilities because it's easier to say "It won't happen to me," "I'm careful" or "I don't work with that type of client." But I'm asking you to face your fears and set aside your denial. I know this can be difficult, but I also know you can do it! Repeat after me: "I CAN do it!" The reward will be less fear, less worry and a greatly enhanced safety system.

Protecting Yourself From Violence During Home Visits by Chris Puls

What do predators want?

Predators prefer an easy target. Their success depends on their ability to select a target that isn't going to hurt them or over power them. So what makes an easy target?

Women make easier targets because they are usually physically smaller than and not as strong as men. If the woman is on the young side she could be more inexperienced at reading men and more trusting. If the woman is on the elderly side she may have less strength to fight. But if you are in between these age groups, don't assume you won't be selected. All women usually have what most male predators want: some money, a nature that is easily dominated and a few desired orifices. Many predators see those three items in a reverse order of importance.

A lack of awareness is another thing predators look for when selecting victims. If they know the target hasn't seen them then a surprise attack is easier. It is also less likely that the person will be able to pick them out of a line-up.

Timid and fearful body language and/or mannerisms are like a neon sign to criminals. It tells them "Here I am! Pick me! Pick me! I won't resist you!" These people are displaying their inner feelings for all to see. They do not display the confidence to over power or effectively fight back. If this describes you, I will be covering many ways you can work on changing the image you are projecting. Even during those times that you still feel timid on the inside, no one will know and you can turn off that neon sign.

The right situation is almost a "must have" for predators. But depending on the crime and the victim's reactions, it might not take much privacy to accomplish their goals. In one such case, a predator selected a store clerk in a mall during business hours. He forced her to the back room and raped her. He hasn't been caught yet, but odds are high that he will attack again. Having a target alone is ideal, like inside a private home. This privacy can make up for a lack of some of the other desired traits.

Added benefits would be things like; someone with their hands full which makes it hard for the target to use them defensively. Someone wearing flashy or expensive jewelry which could indicate money. Even a poor choice of shoes or clothing can attract the predator's eye. The clothing doesn't have to be seductive to be a poor choice. It helps the predator when the clothes or shoes make it hard for the person to run or fight. High heels should be outlawed in my personal opinion. Tight skirts that prevent a full swing of the leg make running and kicking nearly impossible. Skirts make sex crimes easier than pants. It is possible to have a professional, feminine look without endangering yourself.

What I ask you to do is to start to look at things through the eyes of a predator. What do you do that a predator could use to his advantage? When you notice something like that, find a way to change it so that you have the advantage.

What are Predators relying on?

> Humans are the only species to participate so voluntarily in their own victimization.
> – Gavin De Becker

Many predators use ploys to get you where they want you. They rely on your ignorance of those ploys, so that you can't see them for what they are. By learning about the methods used by predators you are "arming your instincts" so they can alert you if someone you meet or know starts to use these to control you.

The goal of a predator *during* the attack (or in some cases the pre-attack) is to cause fear and to control you. He also wants you to be confused about what to do which will cause hesitation. He will try to project such a strong image that you will believe that you have no choice but to do as he says. He's relying on your adrenalin dump to paralyze you.

Some attackers rely on speed and surprise, which can cause an exaggeration of the above effects. Simply by being aware of these predator goals, you can start to lessen their effects. Decide that you will not be scared stiff and will not let him control you. I'll show you how to make that a reality.

Protecting Yourself From Violence During Home Visits by Chris Puls

Understanding the effects of fear

Several things can happen in situations of intense fear or surprise.
- You can lose fine control of your small muscles like the ones in your hands. This can make it difficult or impossible to get a key in a lock or to press the desired numbers on a phone.
- Your hands, fingers and possibly your knees could shake. Visibly giving away your internal feelings of fear.
- Your field of vision can narrow and in some cases may become 'tunnel vision' where you only see what is directly in front of you. You may not see others coming to your aid or the assailant's friends coming to his. You might not notice escape routes.
- Your heart rate can increase and your blood pressure can spike to amazing levels. If you have a heart condition, this can be very dangerous.
- Your mouth may get dry and you will likely have the desire to urinate-- an impulse that may be difficult to control. Even minor stress and fear can trigger this feeling.
- Your breathing increases to almost a pant and can cause hyperventilation, dizziness, numbness in your extremities and fainting. Another possibility is that after an initial gasp, you will hold your

breath causing the same physical effects as hyperventilating.
- It may feel like things are moving in slow motion.
- Your hearing may lessen as well, making things hard to hear or you may experience the opposite effect with every little sound seeming to be very loud.
- Your blood flow is getting redirected to your large muscle groups to prepare them for action. This leaves your hands and face pale and your hands may get cold and clammy.

The good news is that in most cases your pain tolerance skyrockets. Many people fighting for their lives have been seriously wounded and said they don't feel it till well after the fight is over.

Keep in mind that the predator may also be suffering some of these symptoms as well. It may be that they are the feelings he enjoys or it could be the first attack he has attempted causing him to be more nervous.

The first few seconds of an attack are the most chaotic within your mind because it causes a 'fight or flight' response.

It is an automatic response (known as reaction mode), and it is not a thinking response. Take for example the less dramatic 'startle' response to a sudden loud sound. You don't think to yourself "Gee, I just heard something crash, I think I'll jump" it just happens.

This is a self preservation mechanism and gets the body ready to fight or flee so you will not be able to eliminate it completely (and you wouldn't want to.) But you can reduce the amount of time that your body is reacting on autopilot by working on decreasing the amount of time it takes you to recover and regain composure. This will greatly reduce and in some cases eliminate the effects of fear listed above. When you feel you have regained some composure, you are back in "thinking mode" and able to think your way out of a developing situation.

Unfortunately, the natural reaction you have to an attack may not be the best. Often it causes such an overload of chemical and electrical responses and a flood of emotion that your brain and body seem to no longer communicate.

Protecting Yourself From Violence During Home Visits by Chris Puls

Overcoming Fear

So how do you interrupt these natural processes and get out of "reaction mode" and into "thinking mode?"

1) Breathe!
2) Move your hands and
3) Think!

Breathing:
By conditioning yourself to take deep breaths from your belly you will be better able to handle dangerous situations effectively while using the adrenalin for power. These breaths need to be deep and full to release any air that might be trapped in the lungs from an initial gasp. Be sure to exhale fully before taking another breath.

Taking slow, deep breaths:
- Helps oxygenate the blood
- Has a calming effect and prevents hyperventilation and fainting
- Helps counter many of the physical effects of fear and stress
- Helps you get back into thinking mode

Moving your hands (& toes):
You need to move your hands and wiggle your toes if you can. By opening and closing your hands, (or grasping then loosening your grip on something like a steering wheel or handful of fabric) you help pump the blood back into them. This will help re-direct the blood flow back to the fine muscles and help increase your

dexterity. When the blood starts to flow to your fine muscles, it also starts to go back to your brain, helping you think more clearly.

Practice thinking during stress:
This is why it was recommended earlier that you practice working through the adrenalin dump while utilizing self-defense techniques. The more times you are able to maintain focus, and maintain the desired communication between your brain and your muscles, the better you are at keeping a clear path to thinking. You are retraining your brain to handle stress in a more effective way. You will still startle and jump, but your recovery from that reaction will be much faster than people who have not practiced.

Force yourself to think. Where are the nearest exits? Who would you call in an emergency? What could be used as a defensive weapon? Who is around you? Can they help you? How would you get their attention?

These methods are used to train police officers, military personnel, fire fighters and anyone that needs to react quickly and correctly under high stress situations. Even if you are thinking to yourself, "I don't want to be a police officer or military person!" learn to use this to your own advantage so that you can have the edge and be able to think your way to safety. Everything you learn (physical skills, mental skills, etc.) will be more effective if you can maintain thinking mode and avoid "blind panic" (reaction mode).

> The faster you recover your composure and can regain a confident image, the less likely that the predator will continue to select you as his victim.

As with building a muscle, your proper mental reaction to stress needs to be practiced. This is easy to do and life gives you many natural opportunities.
- If you feel stressed, (at work, at home, while driving, etc.) practice taking a few deep breaths- from your belly, not just your chest.
- If something startles you, take some deep breaths and move your hands.
- Envision scary situations in your mind. Practice deep breathing while you think of a safe escape solution. It's important to think through these scenarios all the way to a safe conclusion.
- If you are experiencing fear (difficult driving conditions, a severe storm, a doctor or dentist visit) practice deep breathing and moving your hands and feet. Remain in thinking mode by reading or thinking of pleasant experiences.

The movie method: You can set-up situations for practice by using scary movies. These are a simple and affordable method of safely practicing your proper fear response. These allow you total control over the situation through the use of the remote if things get too intense.

As the spooky music starts and the tension builds, practice taking deep breaths. Move your hands and think of how you would have avoided the situation or how you would get yourself out. If things get too intense, you can always pause the movie to re-gain your composure.

Movies also give you the opportunity to gradually increase the levels of fear you are working on simply through the type of movie you choose and when and where you watch it. You can start with a movie you think will cause minor fear and watch it during the day with the lights on. Gradually work your way toward being able to watch a really scary movie at night, alone, with the lights off.

My encounter with "Frank"

Thanks to my own practice with these methods, I was able to save myself from a knife attack and did not have to kill a man that was off his medication.

I was working as a patrol officer on the West side of Cincinnati Ohio on a warm summer evening. I received a call to respond to handle a person that was off his medication, had a knife and was threatening to kill his family and himself.

Due to the fact that we were short handed that day and I was the only officer not already on a critical incident, I ended up at the scene alone.

When I arrived on the scene, I found a small, older home in a middle class neighborhood. I could hear yelling inside the home as I approached the door. I could see through the frosted glass that someone was standing against the door on the inside. With my gun drawn and my senses about as heightened as they could be, I knocked on the door. A woman burst out and said with fear and panic, "He's in there! He has a knife! Please don't kill him, he's my husband and he's just off his medication!" I sent her to the neighbor woman that had come out of the next house who indicated that she would console the wife.

There was still yelling coming from the house; at least 3 different voices. I cautiously stepped through the door and saw the man I'll call Frank. He was agitated, stomping around the middle of the living room about 10 feet away from me. He was in his 40's, wearing torn jeans and no shirt. I could see his ribs but he looked muscular; wiry. He also had a huge kitchen knife he was waving around as he yelled.

As soon as he saw me he started yelling at the top of his lungs, "SHOOT ME! JUST SHOOT ME!" At the same time I could hear other family members down the hall, out of my line of sight, pleading, "Don't shoot him! He's off his medication!" Amid this utter chaos, I made a radio transmission.

If you have seen the T.V. show COPS then you have probably heard what the typical officer under stress sounds like-- total garble with urgent or frantic tones. Thanks to my prior practice and training in the skills of remaining calm under stress, my transmission is now used at the police academy to demonstrate how it should be done. In my transmission you can clearly hear my words because I'm speaking in a conversational tone (although loudly to be heard over the yelling in the back ground of "SHOOT ME!" and "Don't shoot him!"

I clearly told the dispatcher my car number, that I had the subject at gun point, that he did have a knife and to please expedite back-up. As I went back to trying to calmly talk to this irate and erratic man, I hear my back-up come on the radio and say, "I'm at the district (station house), how to I get there?" Oh joy...NOT!

Now I know I'm really on my own and it's up to me to try to talk this guy back to some form of rationality when what it sounds like he really wants is "suicide by cop." This is the term for people that don't have the gumption to kill themselves so they threaten an officer who will do it for them out of forced self defense. I knew that if it came down to him or me, that it would be me that was going home that night.

As soon as the dispatcher heard the transmission of my back-up, she put out an all county broadcast to let the surrounding county officers know that an officer needed assistance. That also helped pull other city officers in the area off of less critical runs. I knew back-up was on the way but it was still several minutes out. Minutes seem to turn into lifetimes in a situation like this.

I spent the next five and a half minutes talking to Frank and trying to convince him that today was not a good day to die. I was thinking that what I was saying must have worked because by the time back-up arrived, Frank had dropped the knife. Well, let's say it was out of his hand. He had thrown it so hard at the floor that about ½ an inch of the tip was imbedded in the floor boards under the carpet. He was sitting in a chair, still mad but calming down. With a bit more conversation after my back-up arrived, I was able to talk him into voluntarily letting us put the handcuffs on for the ride to the psych ward of the hospital.

This incident had a happy ending, but it's not only the story, but what happened about a month later that helps illustrate the power of remaining in thinking mode under stress.

About a month after this incident, I was driving through Frank's neighborhood on a less hectic day and I saw him in his yard. I stopped to say hello and see how he was doing. He said he was fine and recognized me as the officer that responded when he was off his medication. He told me that he remembered the whole incident. He also told me something I'll never forget.

He said that he had been in Vietnam and he had seen the look that was in my eyes that day. He said he could tell, just by looking in my eyes that I would have killed him if he had made a threatening move toward me. I told him he was right because I knew before I even entered his home that day that I was going to make it home that night. He said he decided that he didn't want to die that day. I don't know if what I had said to him that day helped him reach that decision, but I was very happy that my prior training helped prevent a death; Either mine or his or both.

Just because you are not a police officer does not mean that YOU can't end up in a life or death situation. Your ability to remain in thinking mode and to stay calm may be the deciding factor.

> If you can control your fear responses and recover quickly from "reaction mode" under high stress conditions, you can handle just about anything!

Your first reaction to stress should be deep breathing-- from your belly. The reason is that a startle and fear response will rob you of air. It's like getting hit in the stomach really hard or being stuck under water unable to breathe. Concentrate on your breathing so you can get needed oxygen to your brain so that you don't pass out and you can remain in thinking mode.

By focusing on taking slow deep breaths during your practice sessions, you will be able to better control negative physical reactions within your body. By filling your lungs, you will be able to give louder vocalizations like, "NO!" and "GET AWAY FROM ME!"

Speaking of vocalizations...
Instead of screaming, practice yelling words in low and forceful tones. Get mad! An alternative is to use a battle yell. If you listen to football players as they clash together and people practicing karate you get an idea of the sound you want to make. It comes from deep in your belly and forces your abdominal muscles to contract. This has the added benefit of forming a wall of muscle over your mid-section that can help protect your internal organs from an impact like a punch.

Screaming comes from the lungs and is not a strong sound. People don't react much to screams and due to the high pitch it can sometimes be hard to tell exactly where the sound came from. When you are alone in your car practice your forceful words and battle yells. If you are concerned that someone might see you, pretend you are on the phone. Don't forget to breathe deeply and concentrate on your driving (thinking).

Sometimes fear arises before the first physical contact. Just the look or words from the predator are enough to elicit an automatic response of adrenalin production.

> The faster you recover your composure and can regain a confident image, the less likely that predator will continue to select you as his victim.

Throwing the criminals off guard
It is not uncommon for predators to wait for you in areas where you are not likely to have help. This could be a deserted parking lot, a stairwell or a rural street. I believe I had this happen to me while I was off duty.

As I approached the doorway to a warehouse from a deserted parking lot, I thought I actually recognized the menacing looking man that was standing and smoking a cigarette near the door. I thought he was someone I had arrested about 6 months earlier. My gut tightened; however, outwardly I remained calm and confident. I made the same comments that are suggested below and I found them to be very effective. It turns out that he wasn't who I thought he was but it didn't matter. I was able to get into the warehouse and he left the area. After I was in a safe location, I analyzed why it had worked and vowed to use it again if the need arose.

Later, in the book *Defensive Living* by Bo Hardy, I read about this technique I had already stumbled upon. Here's an example of how you could use this technique:

You have found yourself distracted as you walk out of your client's home. You are thinking about the work you just did and whether or not you had a positive effect on the client. You were not able to park near the client's home and have to walk down the street a little way to your car. Your awareness of your surroundings returns when you finally realize that there is a person leaning against your car and he doesn't look friendly. Of course, you are likely to have a startle response but if you recover from it quickly you can use acting skills to your advantage. You will want to regain your composure and approach with confidence. Make eye contact and smile like you just realized it is someone you know. Say "Greg right? It's been a long time since I arrested you. Have you been staying out of trouble?"

Let's look at what this simple act has done. First, it is the opposite reaction from what he was expecting! Instead of becoming fearful, you are confident. Secondly, what you said *implies* that you are or were in the law enforcement profession without "impersonating an officer."

You are using his assumptions to get you out of becoming a victim. Even though he knows that you are mistaken in your beliefs about who he is, he knows that he obviously looks a lot like someone you know and could thus pick out of a line up. Criminals don't want you to think you know them. What you have done is turn the tables and create the fear and uncertainty in HIS mind! He will likely feel compelled to respond to your statements and that means you get to hear his voice.

In using this technique, the man by the doorway I needed actually said, "I'm not Greg, my name is Tony" as he moved away from the door. He was so thrown off guard he gave me his name!

Disclaimer: I am not telling you to impersonate a police officer or try to arrest anyone. You are simply letting him jump to conclusions so that you can stay safe. Only use it in a situation where you feel you could be in danger and need to do this to escape.

Protecting Yourself From Violence During Home Visits by Chris Puls

Do you look like a victim?

Confident body language puts out a welcome mat for the good guys and a "go away" sign for the bad guys.

Have you ever been about to meet someone and you knew before they even opened their mouth that you weren't going to like them?

Have you entered a room full of strangers and been able to pick out who is preoccupied with their own thoughts, who would be willing to answer a question you might have and who looks as lost as you are?

Because of the body language and mannerisms of people you have never met, you are able to confidently and correctly assess how your interactions with people are affecting them. So, it's not much of a stretch to think that predators can also learn to read subtle body signals to quickly pick out suitable prey or to discount certain people.

In 1984 two researchers, Betty Grayson and Morris Stein, conducted a study to determine the selection criteria predators used when selecting their victims. They videotaped several pedestrians on a busy New York City sidewalk without their knowledge.

They later showed the tape to convicts who were incarcerated for violent offenses like rape, murder and robbery. The researchers instructed them to identify people on the tape who would make easy or desirable victims. The results were interesting.

Within seven seconds, the participants made their selections. What baffled researchers was that almost all the convicts chose the same victims! But the reason a person was chosen was not readily apparent. Some small, slightly built women were passed over. Some large men were selected. The selection was not dependant on race, age, size or gender. Even the convicts didn't know exactly why they selected the people they did. They said some people just looked like easy targets.

To find out why the victims were chosen you need to think like a predator. View the world through their eyes and see the opportunities they see. What these predators were seeing was subtle body language that projected "I am a good victim." I'm going to teach you how to avoid that body language!

> Concentrate on portraying the confidence that you can handle yourself and that you are not afraid. Even if you feel fearful on the inside, pretend you are an actress that needs to play the roll of a very self-assured woman.

As you read on, and as you practice you will find this is easier, because you will have the power of defensive knowledge -- you WILL have that confidence.

Someone with confident body language:

- Smiles
- Has an open posture
- Is relaxed
- Has a purposeful and fluid heel to toe walk (difficult or impossible to do in high heels)

- Keeps her head up
- Her shoulders are squared
- Her back is straight
- She is comfortably aware of her surroundings
- She makes eye contact

Using confident body language is a <u>SKILL</u> that can be learned and turned into a habit. I urge you to work on this every chance you get.

When you
- are at the mall
- are grocery shopping
- are out with friends
- get out of your car
- leave the house or office

> If you are in public, you should be practicing the use of confident body language

Practice making eye contact, displaying confident body language and saying a genuine hello to everyone you can. By doing this, it will come more naturally when you really need it. It has the added benefit of helping you look confident to all those people you practice on and it is possible one of them was evaluating you as a potential victim until you made eye contact and spoke with confidence.

One of the easiest ways for you to project a confident image immediately and "on demand" is to think of someone you know that is very confident. Perhaps it is a public speaker, a police officer, a friend or a person in the military. We are likely to recognize the strength he or she portrays. Now act like *you* are that person. How would they handle the situation that you are in?

Mimic her body positioning, gestures and tone of voice. Practice being that person as often as you can and you will feel the difference between the way she carries herself and your current body language. You can practice acting like several different confident people. The idea is to incorporate their manner into yours so that you can look just as confident as they do and turn it into a habit. Once it becomes a habit, you won't need to think about the behaviors and mannerisms, they will be there for you without conscious thought.

> Anytime you notice yourself acting weak or projecting a victim image, switch to a more confident personality.

Confident self talk is important too. Say to yourself that you are as confident as you are making yourself look. Say to yourself that you can handle yourself and will trust (and listen to) your instincts. Of course, as mentioned above, knowing how to handle yourself in dangerous situations will give you tremendous confidence that will shine through in your day-to-day life. My mission is to give you that knowledge and confidence.

Think about how animal predators choose their prey. They don't go for the strong members of the herd; they look for the weak, old, injured or young because they are easier to bring down. Human predators often do the same thing when selecting their next victim. Learn to use confident body language to avoid looking like easy prey in the human "herd."

By learning what the predator is looking for you can avoid looking like his next victim. Practice self-awareness and the projection of a confident image. Consciously make the effort to walk with your head up and with purpose in your gait. If you believe you are likely to be a victim, chances are that those thoughts are 'showing through' in your body language or speech. Avoid those negative thoughts and instead look for answers to the "what if's" you may be playing in your head.

Find every way possible to combat the fear and doubt that may be preventing you from feeling confident. It doesn't matter if you are only five feet tall and ninety-five pounds soaking wet; if you have confidence it will be evident and will tell others you are to be taken seriously. Even kids can use these methods effectively!

Body language to avoid includes:
- looking down or away
- nail biting, hair twisting, nervous mannerisms
- slouching
- shuffling your feet
- covering your mouth as you speak
- a weak handshake

Make a conscious effort to keep your hands below your neckline if you tend to twist your hair, nail bite or play with your earrings. Instead of chastising yourself for using poor body language, reward yourself for noticing any poor image projection and make an effort to change it to a more confident projection. Don't expect this to happen overnight. Habits can be hard to break. The good news is that once you turn the bad habits into good ones, those will be hard to break as well.

A strong, confident handshake says just as much as a weak, wimpy one -- but it doesn't say the same thing. Which image do you want to project?

Guess which one is more likely to be considered as a victim. If you are worried that a man will give you a "crusher" handshake, consider that it hurts much less if he has his fingers around the 'meat' of your hand (as in a full handshake) than if he just has your fingers.

By using your muscles to give a firm grip, they help protect your hand from the "crusher" grasp. Be sure your firm handshake also includes a warm smile and direct eye contact. If he is gripping too hard, you could say "Easy on the hand please, I hurt it during karate class."

Relaxed eye contact should be maintained while a conversation is taking place. Don't look away or down for more than a second or two as you speak. Avoidance of eye contact when speaking shows submission, uncertainty or meekness. None of these traits will help prevent you from becoming a victim. If the person to whom you are speaking does not maintain eye contact, he may not feel that you are interesting or important enough to warrant his attention or he could be using a shy routine to put you at ease. Of course, he might actually be shy.

Your smile should be genuine. If it is forced or nervous it can be very obvious. If you smile when the topic of your speech does not warrant a smile, it can make it appear as though you are trying too hard to be liked. That can come across as appeasing or mealy-mouthed. Instead, concentrate on having your facial expressions match what you are saying. If it is not appropriate to show your true feelings with your expression then try to keep a 'neutral' expression.

How you speak
Your speech affects how you are perceived. It should be authoritative and confident. Don't start sentences with phrases like: "Um, I was just wondering..." or "This probably isn't important but..." Before you talk to someone about something you are hesitant to discuss, practice asking him about it in different ways.

Go with the one that sounds most self-assured. If it is a touchy subject, you can come across as both confident and sympathetic if you find just the right words and pair them with self-assured body language.

Be sure you are speaking loudly enough to be heard easily. If you are very soft spoken you may need to practice what feels like yelling to you. Practice with friends or family and encourage them to tell you what volume sounds best. It will probably surprise you how loud you need to be to avoid sounding timid.

Pauses in speech are fine. Don't feel like you have to fill them with sounds like "um" or "ah." If someone else pauses when they speak, they may be trying to formulate the completion of their thought. Some people feel the need to always say the right thing and end up with long pauses in their speech-- especially if they have been asked a question. If you fill that silence with another question, it will slow them down even further. Don't feel like you have to fill the silence with your voice.

If you are the type that needs the pauses to think, it will help if you learn to start that thinking process by telling the other person "Let me think about that a moment" or other words or gestures to indicate thought. This lets them know you are thinking and silence would be best. It helps prevent them from assuming you are "slow" or that you have not understood the question.

If a predator is using long pauses in his speech to make you uncomfortable, don't fall for it. This ploy is accompanied by direct eye contact, unlike deep thought when his eyes are likely to wander. Recognize that it is a ploy and accept the pauses without letting them make you appear nervous. Also realize that he is fishing for power and control, so raise your guard.

Hang around confident people and watch how they act and react. Ask any teen and they will tell you it's not what you know, but *who* you know, that is important for your image. Shallow, yes, but in today's society it works. When people project confidence they can help bring it out in others around them. Think of them as motivational speakers; you just need to turn up the volume, using observation, to "hear" their methods.

Trust your instincts

> Intuition is knowing, without knowing why.

This is one of the most important sections of this book. You may not know it, but you already have a strong survival instinct. By being made aware of some of the signals that warn of danger, you will be able to recognize them more easily if you see them.

Intuition is so strong it even works when we are asleep. Many people that say they can sleep through anything, also admit that they wake up immediately if they hear their young child during the night or hear the cat retching in the other room. Your intuition can tell the difference between the sound of glass breaking on the TV show in the other room and the window breaking down the hall and will wake you up for the latter. It's the part of our brain that processes sounds and sights for signs of danger or need without our conscious effort. If something occurs that warrants our attention, the intuition sends signals that let the conscious part of the brain know action needs to be taken.

Hopefully the information I'm teaching you will help you justify and listen to that little voice in your head that is trying to warn you of danger. Ralph Waldo Emerson said the following profound words: "Trust your instinct to the end, though you can render no reason." Even though Jane could "render no reason" for her unease, she should have trusted her instincts.

> **The number one rule for keeping yourself safe is to trust and act on your instincts!**

Call it women's intuition, gut feelings or a sixth sense if you like, but often those feelings are based on very subtle cues you pick up subconsciously. The "Beware of Dog" sign you didn't realize you saw or the man that peeks out of the second floor window as you approach the house of the female client; the client that was supposed to be alone.

Intuition may present itself in other forms as well:
- Persistent thoughts
- Anxiety
- Curiosity
- Hunches
- Nagging feelings
- Doubt
- Hesitation
- Dark humor
- Suspicion
- Apprehension
- Fear

Often we get nagging feelings that someone or something isn't quite right-- something that tells us that we may possibly be in danger. But we ignore the voices and feelings. We even try to ignore the most persistent feeling-- fear. We tell ourselves to calm down, relax, it's probably nothing. We tell ourselves that we are overreacting. We tell ourselves there is nothing to worry about and everything is fine. Please **stop** dismissing those feelings. Listen to them and use them as a reason to explore the situation further. Let them keep you safe as they were designed to do.

Mary was meeting with a client that gave her the creeps. She had asked several of her co-workers to go with her but none of them were able to go. As she left the office, she said jokingly, "That's OK, it's not like he's a killer!"

Turns out that her use of dark humor was right on target. The client killed her that day.

All animals have survival instincts and they always listen to them. You will not see a prairie dog staying around when it sees a hawk because "he looks like a nice hawk." Although we are all blessed with these survival instincts, humans choose to ignore them (or train themselves to ignore them) and often pay the price by becoming victims and statistics.

In Jane's case, there were several subtle signals that her mind perceived on a subconscious level. Later when Jane learned about them, she could easily pick them out of her story. Had she known how to see them as ploys at the time, she most likely would have listened to her feelings and prevented such a horrible, life-changing event.

By the time the hair on the back of your neck raises, you probably need to get away from the situation! Later in the book I will give you ways you can quickly get out of various situations that make you nervous, but that also let you return to work with the client later if you need to do so.

It is important for you to learn to recognize the signals so you don't dismiss your instincts. Developing your instincts in the ways I explain will also help you avoid unnecessary fear and reacting when it is not required.

You may never really know for sure if trusting your instincts saved you from something horrible. This is another reason they are easy to dismiss. You don't get enough positive feedback when your suspicions were correct.

I can guarantee that the uncertainty of not knowing is much better than dismissing the feelings and finding out you should have listened! We suppress the signals so that we aren't rude or wrong, but what could be more wrong than finding out you should have listened?

If you feel like everyone raises your awareness, think of the many encounters that you have with complete strangers that don't arouse any suspicion. The store clerk, the bank teller, the postal employee, the ticket agent at the movies, the group of people you rode an elevator with, your co-workers, most or all of the people attending the theater with you; These are all examples of your intuition at work. Your intuition has learned to recognize normal behaviors, body language and speech. Because of this, it will be more noticeable when you see some of the more obvious warning signals because they stand out. However, many of them can be easily "explained" and dismissed by someone who doesn't recognize them as possible danger signals.

Don't worry about strangers, just strangeness.

Possible physical signals include:
- A stare held too long
- A smile that curls too slowly
- A narrowing or widening of the eyes

- Rapid looking away like you just caught him doing something he knows he shouldn't have been doing
- Following - If someone is following you uninvited, that is a big warning signal
- Getting too close – These people are called space invaders. Ask them to step back or move over
- Inappropriate contact – If it feels wrong, it is
- Hesitation related to lies – Not all criminals are good liars

So how do you know when those feelings you feel are real and when they are imagined?

Real feelings are generated by something in the environment that you are seeing or sensing in some way; Subtle clues that your instinct sees or senses subconsciously. False feelings are based on something you imagine and are generated from within; your imagination at work. By learning how to listen to yourself and honestly evaluate the source, your instincts will be sharpened. You can learn to relax because you'll know that you will be warned if something valid needs your attention. You will be able to minimize or eliminate the generation of false fears by your imagination as well.

> When you trust your instincts, you don't live in fear, you live with confidence.

Drugs inhibit your intuition

Alcohol, illegal drugs, some prescription medicine and some over the counter medicine can have a profound negative impact on your ability to sense danger. These can also affect your motor skills and reduce your ability to defend yourself. Illnesses like the common cold and other more serious illnesses can also affect your senses. If you are taking anything that makes you drowsy or affects your emotions, or if you are not fully healthy, your instincts may be impaired. Only you will be able to assess if this is an acceptable risk you are willing to take.

If your condition increases your risk, you may want to take some time off of work or take another person with you for your home visits. If possible, you may want to reschedule your visiting appointments and work in the office until you can be fully aware.

Because these conditions can affect your perception and motor skills, they can also affect your ability to drive. In some cases, your condition can make it illegal for you to drive; even if the impairment is caused by over the counter medication. If you choose to drive when your senses are dulled or your motor skills are affected, you not only put yourself at risk, but also everyone else that is on or near the road. To paraphrase the billboards and commercials; "Buzzed driving is impaired driving" regardless of what causes the "buzz." The earlier section titled "Attention Employers" goes into some of the possible liability for the company.

Awareness is critical!

To see the signs of developing danger, you have to be alert. If you make it clear that you are aware of who and what is around you, you are less likely to look like an easy target and it helps you spot danger as early as possible. With that said, I don't want you to feel you need to look like a secret service agent protecting the president!

> You want heightened senses, not paranoia.

A casual look around and making eye contact with the people around you is enough. Brief direct eye contact lets others know you see them and conveys confidence. In contrast, we have all seen people that hustle along, looking at the ground or that look around so intensely that you can see their fear. Attackers look for these people.

It used to be thought that if you see someone who looks dangerous, you shouldn't make eye contact. Now we know that is bad advice. If you avoid eye contact, he may think you are not aware of the people around you and he knows you have not really seen his face. Avoiding eye contact has the effect of projecting fear or at least a lack of confidence.

If someone makes eye contact with you, briefly maintain the eye contact in a relaxed way. Quickly averting your eyes gives him the signal that you feel vulnerable; that he makes you feel nervous or afraid. Don't stare, but do make brief eye contact and smile confidently to let him know you are aware of his presence.

Use your awareness to spot nearby safe areas (restaurants, police stations, shopping malls). Before you exit your car, look for any potential hiding places for attackers, both close to the car and closer to the house. The "client" might not have had any intention for you to get as far as the porch.

Watch for any dangerous objects in the home such as fireplace pokers, letter openers, kitchen knives or pans of hot water on the stove. Even a pen or pencil can be a stabbing weapon.

> Anything that could potentially be used by the predator against you, could also be used by you in self defense.

Once you enter, know where the exits are located. Stay aware of where the client positions himself in relation to the exits. Does he attempt to always block them? This will be discussed in greater detail a bit later.

Look for subtle clues that indicate things may not be right. Here are some examples:

- The name on the mailbox doesn't match the name of the client.
- He says he has children, but there is no indication of any toys in the yard or the home.
- He says he lives in one location, but wants to meet in another more secluded location.
- There are "Beware of Dog" signs or other warning signs prominently displayed such as "Trespassers will be shot, survivors will be shot again."
- He meets you in front of the home, but the address numbers don't match the ones you were given.

These are the subtle signals that we might not realize we see, but that make us uneasy. These are the types of things that set off the warning bells and trigger our instincts to alert us.

If you have any concerns about your safety, don't enter the home. If you are already inside the house, use the excuses mentioned later to get out safely or to alert someone that you need help.

Protecting Yourself From Violence During Home Visits by Chris Puls

Warning signals

A wolf has no choice but to always show the predatory tools that make him an effective hunter-- size, muscle, and large teeth contained in powerful jaws. But if he had the option of looking like a little puppy when it suited him, he could be even more effective. Man can do just that. They are masters at disguising their intentions. You have to master the art of seeing through the disguise.

The following signals are not set in stone for every situation. They are meant to provide a base of knowledge you can expand upon with practice and experience. No matter how many I listed, I could never address all the situations you might encounter. By learning to watch for the signals below, you will be miles ahead of your less knowledgeable colleagues and will be able to assess situations for yourself.

Just because someone displays one or more of the signals below does not mean he's a predator. It is likely he wants something from you, but it might not be anything more sinister than some conversation or a simple favor. Many people use the techniques listed below to guide others to a decision (like making a big purchase) or to get them to do something they want (like go out with them). As discussed below, the context of the signal use and your instincts, which are picking up additional signals, will need to be used as well.

Learn to trust your instincts and to practice using them, rather than ignoring them. If the situation allows (or after you are safely away from the situation) analyze why your senses were raised. Look for the subtle signals that you may have missed when you were concentrating on the situation. By doing so, you may learn many things that you can apply to future interactions and it will help train your instincts.

> Always give yourself positive feedback and rewards for listening to your inner voice when it tells you things are not right.

If you miss some signals that you realize later you should have seen, don't punish yourself for missing them. Vow to learn from the experience and move on. You won't miss them the next time.

Out of the ordinary
A big part of recognizing signals that are acceptable and those that are possible warnings is to look at how they fit into the current context. Is what you are seeing normal for this person, in this situation, at this time?

Jane saw some of this, but chose to ignore it. She saw the lack of a wedding ring and identification, the lack of pictures of the kids he was so proud of and she saw his hesitation as he thought of an excuse for not having pictures of the non-existent kids.

Note: It was determined that the odds of him really having kids of his own were low. This is because anyone that does have kids knows that when they come up as a topic in a conversation, the question "Do you have any pictures?" usually follows. When he decided to pretend he had kids to make Jane feel more at ease, he neglected to plan for the question of pictures. The likelihood of him having pictures or a better excuse for the next attack is very high. Criminals learn from their mistakes and perfect their trades just as you and I do.

Later, she saw the uncut grass and lack of curtains, then the lack of possessions in the home even though he said he was living there. This was a big signal that she finally allowed herself to listen to, but it was too late.

Suppose you enter a home and the client you have known for some time is not acting the same as in previous visits. Should you be concerned? Well, that depends on the context of the situation and other signals. If they are exhibiting signs of violence or angry outbursts, you might need to start figuring out how you can get out fast. Perhaps they are not taking needed medication or they have an illegal drug habit. It could be that they are just having a really bad day (it happens to the best of us).

Whatever the cause, odds are high that you will not be able to have a productive meeting until the client gets some medication or some help or calms down.

> Listen to your instincts. What are they saying? If they tell you to get out-- DO IT!

If your instincts are not sending any warning signals, then you can assess the situation to see if there is some way to help the client in spite of the strange mood or behaviors. Maybe you need to say, "I noticed you seem a bit upset. Would you prefer that I come back another time?"

That can give him the opportunity to explain what is going on or to give you the option to leave. His answer may provide additional clues to the seriousness of the situation.

Try not to take things out of context, look at the big picture to get the best feel for the situation. Just because a client does something that might heighten your senses, that doesn't mean you need to instantly run out. Trust your instincts and keep context in mind.

In Jane's case, on their own, the missing ring and the lack of pictures may not have meant any danger. However, when combined with other signals, it all added up in that context to danger signs.

"He was so nice"

Believe it or not, this is often part of the description given of attackers by their victims. Why you might ask? Well, with the exception of violent, unplanned crimes of opportunity, many predators test their victim before committing to the attack.

They may take a distant look by watching the victim for several minutes or several months. They could be looking for patterns, weaknesses, openings or ways to "innocently" make contact with her. Others may find ways to lure the victim to them. Getting her to a place where the attacker can feel comfortable and in control.

One of Jane's coworkers believes she saw Greg watching Jane from across the street through the big window in Jane's office prior to their first contact, but dismissed the feelings that it was odd behavior and didn't say anything until after Jane had been attacked. It is possible Jane had also seen him without realizing it and that was the cause of the initial "bad feeling" at her office.

He used the information she gave him (full name, age, unmarried, general location, etc.) to find out where she lived and probably watched her there too.

You can use your intuition and objectivity to help others as well. If something doesn't seem right, tell the person or people you think would be most effected and let them make their own decision. It can help raise their awareness level and can help validate the feelings they may have already had. Your ability to clearly voice your intuition can help break through their denial.

While I was in the food court at the mall recently, I was "people watching." I noticed a man in his early thirties, in a light weight jacket and lightly tinted glasses, who seemed to be keeping a close eye on a woman and her baby. The more I watched, the more abnormal his behavior seemed to be. It was clear that he was trying to watch her without letting anyone know he was watching her. And he was pretty good at it too.

When she sat down at a table in the food court, he sat down several tables away. I decided not to ignore my feelings and I went a spoke with the young woman. I told her my name and that I was people watching and asked if she knew she was being watched by a man in a tan jacket. She was visibly alarmed by the question and said "No! Who? Where?"

I gave her his description and told her where he was sitting. As soon as she made eye contact with him, he got up and went out an exit door. She was mad. She said "It's probably someone my ex-husband hired to spy on me!" I told her that was a possibility, but not to assume the guy was a detective. I also advised her to get a security officer to walk her to her car when she was ready to leave so she could safely get the baby inside the car seat.

Was the guy a detective? I'll never know. Maybe she won't either. Was there a gun under his jacket? It's possible. If it turns out he was a predator, my simple actions may have saved her from a lot of grief and trauma.

> Predators are likely to engage their victims in conversation prior to attack.

He will use a simple and seemingly "chance" encounter to test you as a possible victim. He could ask you what time it is, if you know the location of some landmark or store or just make comments about the situation or circumstances to see how you reply.

Assuming I hadn't warned her, if the person watching the lady in the mall was a predator and had approached her in the parking lot with a request for simple help like the time of day, I'm guessing that she probably would have spoken to him. The baby already occupied one of her arms, packages occupied the other. Juggling them to look down at her watch might have been the opening he needed. Or maybe he would have been the Good Samaritan and "helped her out."

The purposes of the predator's conversation can be many. He is trying to see if he can:

- See signs of weakness or yielding
- Distract your mind from the real purpose of this interview
- Get your hands occupied as you point out directions or dig for something in your purse he has just requested
- Get you to look away as you give directions or the time.

These can give him the ability to attack if the situation allows or it gives him the information he needs for a later attack if your interview answers or body language qualifies you as a good target.

I know I was targeted and "interviewed" at least once in my life. I was off duty, in street clothes, and not armed near a bank after second shift (around midnight). The bank was located in the inside corner of an "L" shaped shopping strip so it was about as far from the main road as possible on that corner. Admittedly, it wasn't the best location or time to be using an ATM, and it was a walk-up so I had to be on foot, but it was convenient for me. That convenience could have cost me dearly.

As I walked up to the bank two men appeared to be having trouble with the walk-up ATM I had planned to use. They were both average height, average build, white males dressed in jeans and T-shirts. Both looked liked they could handle a set of weights easily. One of them approached me with a seemingly innocent smile to tell me "that darn machine isn't working." He told me that he really needed some cash because he owed a bar tab and asked if I knew where another ATM was located. If my guard had not been raised, he may have seemed like a nice guy having a bad day.

As he spoke, his buddy tried to casually maneuver to walk up behind me. My warning bells were going off, but I changed my position just as casually to keep them in front of me while I continued to use direct eye contact with both of them. I didn't sense that either of them was drunk or otherwise impaired. I told them there was another ATM just down the street and pointed without looking away from them.

They looked at each other then crossed the driveway to get in their van that was parked in the closest parking spot and drove away. I took down their license plate number and description. I immediately called a third shift sergeant at my police station and explained what happened. He ran the plate and found that it was stolen. I suggested that they check near-by ATM's but the van was not seen again. While I was on the phone I tried the ATM, since that was the reason I was there in the first place, and found that it worked just fine.

I have no idea what they had planned, but I know that my casual maneuvering, confident body language and eye contact saved me from something. As calm as I may have appeared on the outside, I was mentally preparing for an attack. I was picking strike targets on each of them and planning how I would move to put them at a disadvantage. I was scanning the area with my peripheral vision to check for help (both theirs and mine). I was making a note of the closest cover in case they were armed and going over a few disarming techniques in my head. I was relaxed, ready and confident that I would prevail. I'm sure that showed. I'm also convinced that if I had shown the slightest weakness that these guys would have attempted to make me a victim in a heartbeat.

If someone approaches you without invitation, he should be under careful scrutiny. Don't let yourself get so involved in a conversation, his gestures or eye contact that you miss his buddy coming up behind you.

A predator may try to charm you, or build a rapport. Sounds like Greg, right? But charm is a *choice* not a character trait. Charm is something he can turn on and turn off as it suits him and it indicates that he has a motive; he wants something. Don't mistake charm and chivalry for good intentions or an indication of a pure heart. Predators (and others) use charm because it works. What he wants may be nothing more than friendly conversation with you, but it could just as easily be a desire for something more sinister.

He may do something nice to make you feel indebted to return the favor. By picking up something you have dropped (or that he 'accidentally' knocked out of your hands) or giving you a compliment or by carrying your bag he makes you feel obligated to be nice to him. It also makes him look nice and safe if you haven't been trained to spot those things as possible ploys and tactics.

If he is carrying an item you need or want, he knows you will follow him or stay with him. If you feel uneasy, decide just how much you REALLY need or want the item he is carrying to "help" you.

Make a conscious effort to avoid getting into situations where you do need help. It creates a perfect opportunity for a "charming guy" to take advantage. If you are in need of assistance, ask a person that is of the same gender as you. If that is not an option, then **you** select someone to help you. It's unlikely that your instincts would allow you to choose a predator.

The power of "We"
Another way people can make a false connection or build rapport is to use the word "we." To create a "connection" between the patient and themselves, caregivers often use "How are *WE* feeling today?" This is an example of the positive use of "the power of we."

It can also be used negatively, but it is very subtle until you learn how to recognize it. Some examples could be; "We need to get that basement organized" or "We need to help my child, he's back here." Obviously, these could be innocent statements that try to make a valid connection, a suggestion of teamwork. However, someone with less honorable intentions may also use them to create a forced partnership and/or to move you where they want you.

If something is clearly YOUR job or task, and another person uses "we," check the context. This is especially important if they are trying to use the statement to move you to another location. It might be a warning signal. Greg used this by telling Jane "We have a house to sell" when he felt her hesitate. He was trying to regain some of the partnership they had established and get her back on track toward the house.

Compelling Statements

Would you feel compelled to respond to the following statements?

- "I doubt you could work with someone like me"
- "I'm sure this is more than you could handle"
- "You couldn't possibly help me"

These may be legitimate feelings expressed by the client and you can be comfortable in honestly answering them. They may also be a way to make you feel compelled to continue to engage in a conversation or relationship you want to end and/or to reveal more about yourself.

If these statements are made after you make it clear that you don't want to work with this client-- beware. They may be attempting to "wear you down" till you give in and continue the "relationship." They are refusing to take no for an answer, which is another signal that is explained in the following pages. The defense against these statements is silence. Leave, hang up the phone, or ignore the person. If you have ended the conversation or working relationship then it's over. Don't get drawn back in because he uses shame or guilt to try to get you to prove him wrong.

This tactic is often used in bad relationships, when kids want things (they learn early on if it works) and between any two people where one wants something and the other doesn't want to give it.

"I promise"

Those two words can be very powerful. If you use them with your clients, you usually have every intention of following through. In many cases you have an unspoken and expected promise with your clients-- you show up when you say you will, you help them to the best of your abilities, you don't go over your projected estimate, and you deliver products in good condition.

These two words become possible danger signals when they are used to continue something you want to stop.

> *Example: You have sensed a few danger signals from this client and have indicated you need to get back to your office. You are not worried enough to bolt just yet. Then you hear, "I just want to show you the back room I told you about and then I'll let you get back to your office. It won't take long-- I PROMISE."*

It is possible the speaker has no intention of following through on his word. He is giving a promise you did not ask for and that was not expected. He may be sensing your hesitation and is using the promise to try to get you to stay. Stick to your decision to leave.

When Jane heard Greg say, "I promise," he was giving this signal. He was trying to regain any trust that may have been lost by his other actions. The other subtle signal was that he didn't want to be seen outside the home. He was trying to get her inside as quickly as possible.

T.M.I. - Too Much Information

Have you ever told someone they just gave you too much information? It's likely that they said something you really didn't need or want to hear. Predators can do the same thing but for a different reason.

When a lie is told, it may sound convincing to you but it doesn't sound convincing to the liar. So he continues to pile on the lies and give you extra information to help convince himself (and you).

Greg did this on a few different occasions. When he was talking about his kids, Jane saw it as a father's love and boasting. When he talked about the new house he gave more details than were needed. Jane wasn't selling him a home so she really didn't need to know the traits he liked about the home. It's interesting to note however, that the traits he did select were warnings on their own; "secluded," and "the neighbor's houses are barely visible."

All these details help the person make a "connection" with their target so they don't seem like such a stranger. If he is telling you all about himself, he may be hoping you'll forget he's still a stranger. If you didn't ask for the information, it's T.M.I.

"No" is not a signal to start negotiations

Most of the above examples also show another major warning signal-- not accepting "no" for an answer.

> Attackers are looking for compliance and control. They refuse to accept that *you* have any control.

If they don't yet have you "where they want you," the denial of your right to say no may be very subtle. They may play on their prior acts of kindness or an implied partnership. They will try to make you feel like you are being mean or ungrateful and will use this to wear you down till you give in.

> The more often they can get you to relent to their control, the more likely they are to see you as an easy victim. If you mean NO, say NO and stick to it!

If you feel bad about being rude, consider for a moment what this person might have planned for you if you go with him or do as he says. This should help you be less concerned about being seen as rude or unprofessional.

You do not have to be using the word "no" for this information to be relevant. This section refers to any denial you give, such as the ones in the previous sections. If you say you can't, won't or don't want to do something that is the same as saying "no." Stick to your decision, especially if he is using the previously mentioned ploys or trying to talk you out of leaving.

Most kids learn that begging, persistence, guilt and threats work to get them what they want. They spend their lives perfecting these techniques regardless of whether their motives are honorable or deceitful. We all grow up seeing these ploys as useful negotiation skills.

> When it comes to your safety, there is no room for negotiation.

Don't negotiate or continue to argue. If you have to say it twice, then he is the one causing the escalation not you. Either stay silent and leave or shout confidently, "I SAID NO!" loud enough for everyone within two blocks to hear you.

If the person goes away (even if they are mad) that is preferable to continuing interaction with someone who may intend to harm you.

> You can not turn an ordinary man into a predator by being rude, but you can become a good victim if you are too nice or timid because predators see that as a weakness.

Body positioning

This can be another warning signal. Where the client positions themselves in relation to you and the surroundings can give you some insight into his intentions.

Take the case of a client that positions himself between you and the door. Defensively, it puts you at a disadvantage and signals vulnerability. Always try to keep your exits clear (and be casually aware of where those exits are at all times). In an emergency, windows are exits too (if they don't have bars on them and are not too far off the ground).

Invasion of your personal space may be a sign of rudeness, a mental condition or a warning. It could also be that the person has a closer "personal space comfort zone."

A predator may get in close proximity to see if you will yield to them and move away. Moving away may seem the easy and polite thing to do, but asking the space invader to "please step back" maintains your assertive position.

Greg used several types of body positioning signals with Jane. When she first got out of the car, he got into her personal space to close the door. He attempted to guide her by the elbow, but she pulled away. He then used body language discussed below to get her in front of him as they went up the walkway. At the front door, he invaded her space again by reaching in front of her. Finally, he put his hand on her back. By doing this, he was able to stop her from backing out when she saw the inside of the house.

Space invasion can take place in any pose and is particularly intimidating if you are in a weaker position. If you are sitting or kneeling and someone stands too close it is a more powerful signal than if you were both standing. Be aware of where the client is in relation to you. Also stay aware of your body position relative to his and do your best to maintain equal positions.

The best defense to someone that is getting too close is to ask them to "please step back." If the person means you no harm, they won't mind the request. If it was a test by a predator to see if you would yield to them, they will notice your assertiveness and that simple request can take you off their target list.

"Body Language"

We see it everyday and process it without even realizing. Lack of it makes communicating by email or written word more difficult and miscommunication more likely.

Body language can speak volumes, even when the speaker isn't.

Becoming better at reading body language, pre-aggression signals in particular, can be very important to your safety. If you have not been exposed to angry or aggressive people, or if you don't know what to watch for, you can miss the pre-attack warning signals (both verbal and non-verbal).

If you have seen a Martial Arts movie or been to a dojo (a Martial Arts training facility), then you have probably seen the defensive stance. Police Officers and boxers are also known to use this position. It can be described as feet at about shoulder width apart (or slightly wider), with one foot slightly in front of the body and the other slightly behind. Typically the person's strong side is to the back. For martial artists, this allows the stronger punches and kicks to develop full power and speed. For police officers, it keeps their gun as far as possible from anyone they may be confronting. It is a comfortable and very stable position from which the person can move in any direction easily.

If you see your client adopt this stance and you are uneasy with them due to other signals, you might want to take a step back or try to get them to sit down. You could also move to a place where you have something between you like a table or a chair. This can be a subtle move on your part. If the client means you no harm they might not even notice it. If they do mean you harm it will be very clear that you are aware of that possibility and are taking measures to avoid it. Making this simple adjustment may be all it takes to convince him that you are not an easy target and not worth his effort.

If there are enough other signals, seeing him adopt the defensive stance may be the signal that an attack is about to happen and it is time to get out as quickly as possible. You could say your phone is vibrating and you need to take the call (see the "How to get out" section that's coming up)

Fidgeting or acting in a very nervous and agitated manner can also be a signal. It could mean that the person is simply nervous, or that they have a mental condition, or it could mean they are off their medication and possibly unpredictable. If you take on the responsibility of working with people that need medication to have a more normal life, you need to be very clear and upfront with them about that medication. Don't be shy about making sure they have taken it before you arrive. If you are not sure about his condition you can ask him if he is nervous. How he answers can give you additional information to help you assess the situation.

Clenching and unclenching fists is a big warning sign if there are other aggression signals. If the behavior is not a result of Turettes Syndrome, the person could be volatile and on edge. However, this is also a recommended method of getting blood flowing to the fine muscles of your hands, so maybe he's just nervous and has heard of this method. The differences between nervous and volatile should be plainly obvious.

Facial expressions can say a lot. Learn to read the moods of others by watching their expressions. If you can't concentrate on facial expressions when you are with others, watch people on TV.

> By making a conscious effort to recognize the more subtle signals, you will have the knowledge on a subconscious level when your intuition needs it.

A few of the more common signals were listed previously, but I'll repeat them here. A stare held too long, a smile that curls too slowly, a narrowing or widening of the eyes, rapid looking away, following, getting too close, inappropriate contact and hesitation (thinking of lies) can all be warning signals.

There have been studies done on signals called "micro bursts" that may be picked up by us subconsciously. These are very quick, subconscious appearances of the person's true expressions shown when they are using false facial expressions to hide their real feelings. Typically, video is used and played at a frame-by-frame speed to catch these fleeting signals. Perhaps Jane saw a micro burst or two when she first met with Greg in her office.

Arms folded across the chest can mean that the person is not receptive to your ideas. If it is combined with the 1000 yard stare, you need to get out-- fast. The 1000 yard stare is an instantly recognizable "look" in which the person seems to look right through you to a spot about 1000 yards away (see photo to the right.) He is not hearing a word you are saying, he is busy formulating an attack in his mind or envisioning all

Photo courtesy of Massad Ayoob

the damage he would like to do to you. If this is combined with the defensive stance and a bad attitude you should already be headed for safety.

If you get into a heated argument with someone and they start to turn away, you should take a step away from them immediately. In my career as a police officer, I saw this move several times. It is often a pre-attack bluff used to make you think he is going to walk away, but instead, it is a "wind up" for a punch that is hidden as well as a baseball pitch. After failing to recognize this maneuver the first time I saw it, being a hair too slow to fully react and having it result in a nice bruise on my cheek, I learned to anticipate this move. By the way, it did not get the aggressor out of being arrested but it did add a few more charges.

A person pulling on their ear is unconsciously showing doubt. You can use this as a signal that you need a stronger "sales pitch" for what you are trying to accomplish. Be aware of your own body language if you do not believe what the client is telling you or if you need to use one of the excuses later in the book.

If the client is agitated and he closes his eyes and pinches the bridge of his nose, it can show he is experiencing inner conflict. This could be a very innocent signal or in the case of a mental imbalance, could be a warning that the instability is getting worse. He could be saying to himself, "I really wish she would be less confusing" or he may be thinking, "Should I attack her now or wait for a better opening?"

Tone of voice can be very telling
Yelling is usually a clear sign of anger or agitation. But if someone is making threatening statements, it can be even more disconcerting if he uses a soft, quiet voice than if he were yelling, especially when combined with hard eye contact. This was exhibited when Greg whispered his threat to Jane.

Words said through gritted teeth demonstrate that the person is attempting to control their anger. How long they can continue to hold it is unknown. Even something that one person sees as an innocent expression can be threatening to someone else based on the context and tone.

A social worker was called in to investigate claims of child abuse. The father was upset and voiced his anger about the "false accusation." When the social worker mentioned that children can be removed from the home if there is sufficient evidence of abuse or neglect, the father said with a smile on his face, "If anyone tried to take MY kid, I'd cut their heart out with a spoon."

When the social worker told him threats are dealt with seriously, the father said, "I was ONLY joking!" as if it should have been obvious. But it wasn't as obvious as he may have thought. It turns out that there wasn't any evidence of abuse that could be found so the social worker didn't have to find out if he really was joking or if he was serious in his use of dark humor.

Fights in the household
This would be a very obvious warning signal. If during the course of your visit any type of escalating verbal

aggression or any physical aggression is displayed, excuse yourself and get out as quickly as possible.

Examples of this might be violent arguments between family members or friends, or aggressively acting out due to a missed medication or a mental condition.

People are not thinking in a rational manner at these times and you can't expect to be able to have a productive meeting with them. Even if you are trained to handle these types of outbursts, you should never try to do so alone.

About the warning signals
Once the preceding cues are pointed out as possible danger signs, they become some of the more obvious. Learn to recognize them and see their context.

The information presented is directed at visits to people's homes (or the private places they choose for a meeting.) This is probably a place the attacker feels comfortable and in control. But the information can be used in all aspects of your life. Just because you are out on a blind date or sitting in a coffee shop does not mean the defensive knowledge in this book does not apply.

Use every opportunity you can to observe and learn from other people's body language, speech and positioning and learn to spot abnormal behaviors that could be warning signals. Watch for the signals in people you talk to, in actors on TV and in others you observe from a distance. The more practice you have at seeing them, the more obvious the signals will be in the predator.

> If a person who means you no harm gets rebuffed with a curt answer, he will not turn into an attacker.

He may not think of you as the nicest person, but you don't have to worry that being rude to him will cause him to turn into a predator if that was not his intention in the first place.

Women are expected to always be nice and if they aren't, they are thought of as a 'b.b.i.t.c.h.' but you can think of this as "Bad Boy, *I'm* Taking Control Here." I would rather be called a name or lose a client because I mistakenly saw someone as an attacker than to ignore my intuition and get hurt or worse.

You may think that most people wouldn't hurt you because you know where they live. It is correct that **most people** won't, but it only takes one person looking for a target or off their medication to change your life for the worse or even end it. By making home visits, you can find yourself in a secluded area or at a vacant house or in a crime-ridden area of town. The client may be innocent but the location can set you up for crimes by others.

Jane's case is a perfect example and there are many more. Just because someone tells you his name and presents a home he says is his, does not mean that he is being honest. A situation in which the home ownership is false would be very rare, but it is one of the possibilities you can keep in the back of your mind.

Protecting Yourself From Violence During Home Visits by Chris Puls

False indicators

Going back to the first indicator, context, there are some possible false indicators. Knowing about these possibilities can make you better equipped to make an educated assessment of the situation.

Mental Conditions
The actions of people with certain mental conditions can be very disconcerting if you are not prepared to deal with them. I have listed a few examples, but it is by no means an all-inclusive list. If there are certain types of mental conditions that your job is likely to expose you to, I suggest that you do some research about them. An example of this would be the job of Professional Organizer. Persons with ADHD or Chronic Disorganization are not going to behave the same way as the over worked mother who has simply let the clutter get out of control.

Once again, this illustrates how knowledge is power because it can help you handle the clients and teach them the skills they need in a way they can understand.

The examples given below are signs of the various disorders that are present <u>without</u> medication and could affect the home visitor. There are, in some cases, additional signs and symptoms. In many cases, if the person is on his prescribed medication, you may not know that a disorder exists.

Antisocial Personality Disorder
- Irritability and aggressiveness
- Physical fights or assaults

- Reckless disregard for the safety of others or themselves
- Consistent irresponsibility
- Repeated lying, use of aliases or conning others for personal profit or pleasure

Attention Deficit Hyperactivity Disorder (ADHD)
- No attention to detail, makes careless mistakes
- Difficulty in sustaining attention
- Often fails to follow through on instructions
- Difficulty being organized or keeping tasks organized
- Easily distracted from a task
- Fidgets or squirms in their seat or can't sit still
- High drive or excessive energy
- Often talks excessively
- Very impulsive
- Avoids activities that require sustained attention

Bi-Polar Disorder:
During mania:
- Inflated self esteem
- More talkative than usual
- Racing thoughts
- Increased agitation or activity

During Depressed phase:
- Loss of interest
- Fatigue
- Feelings of worthlessness or excessive guilt
- Poor concentration or indecisiveness
- Recurring thoughts of death or suicide

Schizophrenia:
- Delusions
- Hallucinations

- Disorganized speech
- Catatonic behavior (no apparent awareness)

Tourette's Syndrome:
- Repeated and sudden outbursts of inappropriate vocalizations
- Repeated, sudden physical movements

Learning Disabilities (Many different types)
This can include difficulty with:
- speech
- writing
- reading
- numbers
- motor skills
- processing of visual images

Cultural Differences
Other problems that may be encountered that might send the wrong signal are cultural differences and personal preferences. It helps to be aware of these so that you don't accidentally offend someone and you are not made uneasy by his or her innocent actions.

- *Personal space*

Some cultures, nationalities and individuals do not allow as much space between themselves and the person to whom they are speaking. If you are not comfortable with the lack of space between you and the client, simply say "Excuse me, could you step back a bit?"

- *Physical contact*

Some cultures, nationalities and individuals do not have the inhibitions to touch and contact that most

Americans have. They may put an arm around your shoulder, hold your hand, kiss your cheeks (even with a person of the same sex), etc. If you are made uncomfortable with this you could let them know.

You might say "I would prefer you not do that." However, because it is not done as a threat, social pressure may dictate that it be tolerated.

- *Eye contact*

In some cultures direct eye contact can be disrespectful. You can take clues from the client. If they are not making eye contact, and you can't see any other reason that would cause this, like shyness, perhaps you should also avoid direct eye contact.

- *Women in business*

Not all cultures have or accept women in business. This could cause issues between you and the client if you are a woman. If there seems to be too much of a conflict, you may want to have a male colleague or co-worker step in to keep the client or you may need to tell the client you can't help him.

Your gender could also cause issues and confusion in the client. If you are the first woman he has worked with, he might not know the proper etiquette. His handshake could be rough or it may make him uncomfortable to shake hands and/or he may try to engage you in 'small talk' as he would a male, talking about family and marriage status.

- *Non-verbal signals*

It has been said that some people from India have a hard time saying 'no' to anything. So he may be nodding his head yes indicating something is OK, when it really isn't.

Bowing to someone who follows his or her Japanese culture can be respectful if done properly. The deeper the bow, the higher respect you are showing to them. Dropping your head quickly and briefly toward your chest while maintaining eye contact is like a "mini bow" and signifies agreement with respect.

Avoid using overly expressive facial or hand gestures. Pointing and other common hand signals may be considered rude or have other meanings to some cultures or individuals.

For additional information, especially if you travel a lot or work in areas where a certain ethnic group has gathered, you can search the web for "International Business Culture tips".

Protecting Yourself From Violence During Home Visits by Chris Puls

The "What If's"

In the following section, I have come up with some plausible scenarios. They are situations that have the possibility of occurring in the home visit situation. There are many reasons people visit client's homes or personal spaces, so some of these situations may not apply to your field.

> It is my intention to help you begin to look at the possibilities and try to think of how you would handle the situation.

In this section, I will help you realize that you CAN formulate a plan of action to keep yourself safe. As you read through these situations and the possible plans that follow each one, use the knowledge as a base from which to draw.

By doing so, you learn that if you think of (or are faced with) a situation that is not listed, you will be able to create your own survival skills.

Think about each of the following situations for a moment before you read the solution. Chances are it may have never occurred to you that these might be predicaments in which you could find yourself. See if you can think of a safe solution before you read my suggestions. This will help you practice thinking about your safety and possible solutions.

You may have already experienced one or more of these situations. It may have resulted in an unpleasant or criminal event and when you read the next section you will find how the situation may have been handled better. Keep in mind that you could only use the information you had at that time. You should not second guess yourself or berate yourself for not handling it better.

Crime is not the victim's fault.

This is also important for people that hear others recount things that have happened to them. Don't be quick to judge her, or say "well, you should have just..." She didn't know that at the time and it is inconsiderate to make her feel she didn't do something as well as she possibly could have. Instead, let her know she did the best she could have done at the time, but that in the future, there are things she can learn to give her the power and control to possibly prevent an incident from happening again.

One of the best survival skills you can have is believing you will survive and be OK.

If you give yourself permission to truly believe and don't let the fear overwhelm you, but instead let it guide you, you will have the power to act in whatever way is necessary to make that belief a reality.

Let the fear guide you.

Fear causes some amazing things to automatically happen inside us. As mentioned earlier, you get heightened senses, you get the power of adrenalin, and your brain and body go into "fight or flight" mode. All of these things can help you get out of a bad situation-- or they can paralyze you.

Just as I was able to handle a suicidal and homicidal, mentally unstable man that was armed with a knife; if you know how to control the fear and you have the knowledge you need to formulate a plan, it will help prevent you from freezing or freaking in panic.

The least expensive and most effective way you can protect yourself against crime and hazards is to learn how to be prepared. Have a plan that you know you can and will use if the situation occurs.

Now let's take a look at some possible solutions. The solutions offered below are only some of the possibilities and options available. They may not work for all people in all situations. They are offered as a means of education to build upon so you can create solutions that work for you.

In almost all the situations, you will need to look at the context of the situation for additional clues to determine if there is a threat or if you can wait for more information to make a judgment. When you are creating your own plans of action remember to keep them as simple as possible. The more complex the response, the more likely it will be to go wrong.

1) You realize the client is drunk or apparently on illegal drugs.

Obviously, you will not be able to have a productive meeting with this client while he is impaired. It may be easiest to use one of the general excuses in the "how to get out' chapter. If you imply or out right tell the client it is because of his alcohol or drug use, it could cause a violent outburst and likely denial. People that are intoxicated or 'high' can be very dangerous and unpredictable. His inhibitions are lowered and he may be comfortable doing things he normally wouldn't consider. You need to get out as quickly as possible.

2) The client is very controlling of where you go and when you go there

This could be very subtle or very overt. Some people are masters at manipulating others without them even knowing that the manipulation is taking place. It could be a very innocent act, or a type of personality (not necessarily threatening) or it could be a way to get you where the attacker wants you.

Context is important as are other clues given by the area and the person(s) you are dealing with. If you notice that your client or others in the house are controlling where you go and how you move within the space, look for more clues to determine if it warrants alarm. Trust your instincts! The more subtle the deception, the harder it is to trust your instincts.

If you are not sure, but you want to get out, try one or more of the statements or suggestions in the next section that allow you to later contact the client and re-evaluate, to go back with another helper or to send in another person to help this client.

I'm sure it is now easier to spot how Greg was controlling Jane's movement from the car to the home. He used body positioning and body language in conjunction with the controlling statement "After you" to get her to walk in front of him.

3) The client answers the door dressed in a robe and there is soft music playing in the background with candles for 'mood lighting'

This would be a fairly obvious situation if you are meeting the person for the first time and you are not in the 'personal relaxation services' business. I would not even get in the door with this client. Tell him or her "It looks like I have come at a bad time for you" and LEAVE.

It may also be that the client undresses while you are in his or her home. This person may have a very warped view of your relationship. You need to be very blunt and clear in telling the client that you HAD a business relationship only, but due to obvious miscommunication, you have decided that has come to an end. You can say this as you are leaving.

Another option: As soon as you see the situation starting to unfold, you can wordlessly pick up your things and exit the house. As you leave, make it clear you want NO further communication with the client; simply say, "Do NOT call me or contact me again-- ever." After that, have NO further communication with this person either personally or through friends or coworkers. Do not even respond to tell him or her to bug off-- again-- because any communication may be seen in his or her warped mind as evidence of your continued love.

If you fear violence from him (or her) use one of the excuses in the next chapter and get out. You don't have to wait for a reply once you use an excuse. Don't let yourself get drawn into a conversation if the client uses a "compelling statement" like the ones listed in the warning signals chapter. This client has crossed a line with his or her behavior and you don't need that client. If stalking behavior begins, contact the police.

If you have any of the incidents listed in this section that make you uncomfortable, be sure to document the incident with as many details and exact conversation quotes as you can. Create this report as soon as you are safe and while facts are still clear in your mind. Write down every fact you can think of because what might not seem relevant now, may become relevant later. Be sure to include the date you wrote it and indicate how much time elapsed between the incident and the writing of the report. If the case goes to court two years later, you will be glad you included as many details as possible. Regardless of how clear the incident is in your head after it happens, time will fade many of the details; Having a report that you wrote right after the incident to refresh your memory before or during trial is a huge asset and helps strengthen your case.

Claims of rape are possible whenever you are alone with a client. Having another person with you can help prevent these claims. Men are more commonly accused of this than women. Another possibility is to carry a tape recorder and have it running at each job. Save the tapes for a few months, then you can re-use them.

Depending on the number of clients you see, it may be cost prohibitive to do so for all clients, but you can carry it hidden in a pocket in case you find yourself with a client that becomes strange. The new digital recorders are very tiny, but there is no permanent record like a tape. You could use a digital recorder and transfer only the questionable client meetings to tape.

Unfortunately, the one that accuses you of rape may be the last person you would expect. It is likely that she was acting just as normally as your other clients and the accusation will come as a complete surprise. Keeping detailed time records can also help disprove claims. If you can show that you would not have had the time to assault the client, it will work in your favor.

Be aware of anyone keeping you in the home with conversation longer than you need to be there to get your work done. Always be professional and don't let yourself get too personal with your client if your job does not call for the collection of personal details.

A talkative client that wants to tell you all about herself or asks personal information about you when you are there to do a repair or other non-personal work could indicate trouble. She may be trying to make YOU seem like less of a stranger so a claim of rape is emotionally easier. She can claim you went out with her and told her all about yourself when in reality you never saw her again. Most false claims of rape are about money. She wants the company to settle the lawsuit she files. She really doesn't care that the claims have caused you to lose your job or go to jail. Another possible reason is a mental imbalance that causes her to really believe it happened.

Regardless of the reason, an audio tape of the visit or a second person of your choosing in the room with you can help dispute or eliminate the possibility of false charges. If your co-worker is of the same sex as the client, that will help even more. A man and woman making a home visit to a single female would be less intimidating to her than two men.

4) You have your first contact with a client, a phone call, and already the hair on the back of your neck is going up.

Having a less personal contact with a client, such as a phone call, prior to meeting him at the time and place of his choosing is a very good idea. Another even better option, if possible, would be to meet him in a public place or your busy office first. This allows you to assess him with much less risk to your safety.

It also allows you the opportunity to see if there are any true compatibility issues and if you will be able to help him. An additional benefit is that more people see his face and could possibly identify him later. Make it a habit to introduce your client's to your boss or co-workers for this reason. This meeting would be when you collect his personal details and preferably a copy of his driver's license or other picture identification.

If you are meeting in a location without access to a copier, you could have the client bring his own photocopy of his identification and then compare it to the original.

Verify Client information
If it is possible to verify information he gives you, do it! Don't take his word without checking what he says.

It is sad that it has to be this way, but you can wish for a better world all day long and it won't protect you.

Look him up in the phone book, call him back to check the phone number, make sure the information he gives you matches information he provided on other forms or to others in your office. You could even require him to show picture identification such as a driver's license that you can copy and put in the file kept at your office.

Had Jane done some additional checking on her attacker, it may have raised her suspicion to a level she couldn't ignore. At the very least, it may have encouraged her to take a co-worker with her.

Ask for the client's identification if possible. If seeing his identification is not company policy, maybe it should be. Jane's firm does require a client to show his identification, but when she asked Greg for his, he said it had been stolen. She chose to believe him and "let it slide" rather than asking for other items with his name on them, like credit cards or membership cards. If he says his wallet was stolen, you can ask if he has anything with his name on it like a vehicle registration form or insurance card.

These items would not be ideal because they could be forged, but it is better than nothing. If he is unable to produce anything your guard should be substantially raised.

There are on-line databases available to anyone that is willing to pay for access. Some databases are restricted to companies and businesses but many others are available to anyone. These databases include quick access to any public records such as birth certificates, arrest records, property deeds, driving records, court records and more. It might be valuable to have your organization or firm get access to one or more of these services so client information can be verified. It is also helpful in most cases to know the past arrest record of someone you will be working with privately. If he has past convictions for rape, felony assault, drugs, weapons charges or domestic violence that can provide a good reason to take an additional person with you for safety. All conviction records are public. Just because you know about his past does not mean you need to tell him you know. Many employers are finding these services are a valuable tool and time saver when hiring new people too.

Obviously, information such as a person's arrest record is simply that-- information. How you use that information is up to you. Although I know people can change, if I were about to work with someone that had a recent history of arrests for violent offenses, I would be taking a partner with me!

> You may think that it is rude or unprofessional to require a copy of the identification, but in post 9-11 society getting asked to show identification is such a common occurrence that most people won't even think of it as unusual.

If someone questions the need for the showing of his identification you can let him know it is for your safety and that the files are kept private (and they should be).

If you work in an office where multiple people can access all the files you may want to talk to your boss about having a locked cabinet with limited access for the identification copies and other sensitive documents.

One person could be in charge of filing them to reduce the access to that information by people that really don't need to see it. Be sure that keys to the files are available to at least one other trusted person. If an emergency occurs when the primary person takes a day off, you don't want the police to wait till she can be found before they can get the info they need!

Restricting the access to sensitive information can help keep your clients safe from people within your office that could be tempted to use the information for less than honorable uses. This could include selling the information to others such as solicitors or criminals. Not everyone is as nice or law abiding as they may appear, even your friends or co-workers. Identity theft is big business so it is not uncommon for the information leak to be from inside a company. Marketing companies and thieves will pay for information on possible targets. Unscrupulous or desperate people may simply see this as easy money they can get without hurting anyone.

How many times have you seen a news interview of someone close to a person accused of a violent crime? They almost always say the same thing, "He was so nice, and I never would have thought he could do such a thing." I'm not suggesting that everyone should be suspected. I am trying to alert you to the rampant prevalence of crime to reduce naivety. The more knowledge you have about possible crimes and the way they are committed, the better armed your instincts will be.

> The photocopy of the identification should not be kept with the file you take to the client's home.

It should be in a location where it can be accessed by the person you would call for help in the event of an emergency. The police will want to see it if you are missing or held hostage.

If you work from home or in a small private office, you are responsible for the safety of confidential files. Be sure they are protected from theft, tampering and fire.

Any phone contact with a new client should include the gathering of information that is verifiable by other means. Even if you only have a name and an address, if the person owns the home, you can verify it by checking the county property records; most of which are now on-line.

If he is renting in an apartment complex that has an office, you can call the office and say you need to mail a surprise gift to the client but you can't read your writing. Give the client name and two possible apartment numbers. It is likely that the office clerk will verify one of them or tell you no one by that name lives in those apartments (a warning signal).

If you sense something is wrong during these initial contacts, it is much easier to distance yourself from the client than if you ignore those feelings, set up a face to face meeting and put yourself alone with him.

Again, trust your instincts. If you sense danger, there is something you are picking up on that you may not even be aware of on a conscious level. Let the client know that you can't help him. You could recommend someone who can if you prefer. If you have no choice but to meet with this person, **take someone along with you.** Even if that person is not an employee and just waits in the car for you, it gives you some added safety.

You can tell the client that the person was nice enough to drive you to the meeting when your car broke down and that they are going to wait for you. If the client has no ill intentions, they are likely to be impressed that you would go to such lengths to keep the meeting. If they had ill intentions, the friend in the car may have just taken you off his target list.

If your friend is invited in, use your best judgment as to whether they will be of more use inside the home where the possibility of over powering both of you exists, or if they are better staying in control of a means of escape for you both.

5) You find that the location where your client wants to meet is in an area that you are not comfortable visiting

Let's face it there are parts of almost every city that are less than appealing. It could also be that the location where the client wants to meet does not fit with the job.

If you are a realtor and someone contacts you to sell his home but he wants to meet you at a warehouse nowhere near the home site you may want to reconsider. If you know that the location is undesirable when you make the appointment, you have a few options.

For sites that don't make sense, such as the example above, get more information. WHY does the client want to meet there? Do they work there? Can you verify that with a phone call? If the site is not relevant to the job, decide that you won't meet there and you choose the location for the meeting. If you give the client some form of "NO, I won't meet there" are they willing to accept it?

If you find out the meeting location is less than desirable when you arrive, and the client has not seen you arrive, you can leave. You can make an excuse later. It gives you the opportunity to reassess the situation. Maybe you just need someone to come along with you. If that's the case, tell the client your car broke down or you got sick and need to reschedule.

If you know you can't comfortably work in the client's area or space, let them know. There is no reason to waste both your time and the client's.

Another possibility is a home that looks nice on the outside, but has an interior that should be condemned. The best course of action is to let him know that the job is more than you are willing to handle or that you are not comfortable with the conditions. If you feel you need some assistance from your co-workers for this job, let him know that you need to reschedule to a date that works for everyone that will be involved. See situation number 18 about *hazardous or appalling living conditions* or the *unsafe or unsanitary living conditions* section (under *"other conditions"*) for more information.

6) You find weapons or illegal items in the client's home.

In the case of weapons, the seriousness of the situation will depend on the context. Are they displayed in an artful way? Or are you reminded of the movie Deathtrap? Are they readily available to the client, such as a knife sitting on a kitchen counter or a gun on a bedside table?

> Avoid making requests that get the weapon into the person's hand, such as "Could you put that away?"

Instead, use body positioning and movement to draw the client away from the item or to keep yourself between the client and the item. For example, in the case of the gun on the nightstand, move the client to another room, then determine if you can still work with the client knowing that there is an available weapon in the next room.

You may need to work very hard to control the body language and facial expressions you show when you see a visible weapon. Remember to think "I can handle this. I just need to move him away from it calmly."

A trick I'll mention again in the next chapter is to leave something by the entry door. It can be your coat, a bag or a briefcase. What this does is give you a plausible reason to get to the door. If the client were to start acting strangely, or excuses himself to the bedroom where the gun is, you can go to your item by the door and be ready for a quick escape. If it turns out that there was no cause for alarm, you can continue your business.

Weapons can be a real hazard for professional organizers that are going through the property of clients and helping them sort things. Realtors and designers also tend to open closets that a client might not expect would be opened. You never know what might be uncovered.

It obviously poses a serious risk, especially in the case of blades that may be hidden in the clutter. If you think this is something that you might be faced with, it is in your best interest to ask the client if there might be anything in the area where you will be working that poses an unseen hazard (weapons, chemicals, unstable items that could fall, breakable or broken glass, etc.)

I advise that you ask before you open things such as closets or containers. You could request that the client open them for you.

Some people have a serious aversion to weapons of any kind. If this describes you, you will want to let the client know that you cannot comfortably work with him while the weapons are in the home. Perhaps a solution can be worked out to get the weapons out of the home during the meetings or perhaps you need to suggest he find another person to work with him.

In the case of criminal evidence or illegal items, you do not want to ignore them, but depending on the context you may not want to let the client know you have seen the items. If it is obvious that you have seen the items and you choose to ignore them and work with the client anyway, there is a possibility that you could be charged with failure to report a crime, particularly if the possession of the items constitutes a felony.

This could be a very serious situation and I suggest you excuse yourself as quickly as possible. If it helps you get out, you can tell the client that you don't intend to report it (even if that is a lie). Say that the presence of the items makes you too uncomfortable to continue.

> Your safety is the number one priority. You are not the one that chose to break the law so don't put yourself in a situation where you are held accountable for the client's illegal activities.

You may want to check the laws in your state regarding the reporting of a crime. Having been a police officer and knowing that different officers have different levels of understanding about the specifics of the laws, I encourage you to read for yourself the law or laws that pertain to crime reporting. The laws of most states are on the Internet these days. You can do a search for Your State Law or Your State Statutes, then a search of those results for "Crime Reporting."

If you live or work in a big city, your city may have laws that are more strict than state law, so be sure to check those as well. You can check both the city and state laws by going to your local police station and requesting a copy of the laws that would apply.

If you choose not to report the crime and it turns out that the client was under surveillance, you may have some explaining to do. You could also be implicated if your fingerprints are on the items collected by police or found in the area of the items during a later investigation.

7) While you are visiting, a fight between the client and another person erupts

This can be a very volatile situation. It is not one where I recommend you stay. As soon as you see things start to get out of hand, you need to excuse yourself and get out.

Don't take no for an answer. I have seen first hand how quickly arguments can escalate to violence and the people are not thinking rationally at that point.

If a person has a serious conflict with another person, they are not likely to be able to return to business anyway.

They will be thinking about what just happened, not about the task you are there to accomplish. Excuse yourself and if the situation warrants it, reschedule with the client after he or she has had an opportunity to calm down.

If things seem to be escalating toward violence, you should notify the police after you are safe. As with the above situation, failing to report a crime (if you see or suspect one) could make you liable if there is a serious injury or death.

8) The client is showing signs of not taking a needed medication.

This is another situation where you need to excuse yourself and get out. If the client has not taken medication that he needs, he cannot have a productive meeting with you.

If you are there because you have been called to help him, you should not be there alone. Be sure you have at least one other person from your profession there to help you. Family members of the client don't count as "back up" for you. If things get ugly, the family cannot be expected to jump in to save you. More often than not, they are going to do what they can to protect their family member; Even though they may have been the one that called you to help that family member in the first place.

Any police officer can tell you that in domestic disputes, ALL family members (even the victim) have to be watched carefully for violence toward the police, not just the main suspect.

9) The client threatens you or is verbally abusive

Again, you need to get out and do so quickly. You do not have to put up with abusive behavior or threats from him.

If he is not happy with what you are doing, then you obviously do not have a productive working relationship and there is no point in staying.

In the case of health professionals with clients that do not appreciate the required care that is being given, you will need to judge for yourself the volatility of the situation.

Not all threats and abuse from patients are cause for concern, but just because the patient is ninety years old and bedridden doesn't mean he couldn't hurt you if he really had the desire.

> There are different types and levels of threats, but all should be reported to the police or a supervisor immediately.

There are three main types of threats; direct, conditional and veiled.

- A "Direct Threat" would be "I'm going to kill you." Direct threats are illegal and should be reported to the police as soon as possible.
- A "conditional threat" could be, "If you report me, I'll kill you." The threat hinges on another action, but this doesn't make them much less dangerous.
- "Veiled Threats" are more subtle, such as-- "I'll see you later, I know where you live." Depending on the situation, a veiled threat may not give police enough to create a crime report, but they should still be notified. If the client later shows up at your home, the police then have reason to suspect ill intentions. It also helps document the client's activities.

Be sure to insist on getting a copy of any incident or crime report and file it with your boss along with your own account of what happened.

10) Another person at the home (not the client) is doing something that makes you uncomfortable.

The offending person could be an intoxicated family member, a person making rude comments, someone that is saying things contrary to your work or anyone you don't feel comfortable being around.

Perhaps this other person is giving some of the warning signals mentioned earlier or you are simply not comfortable with being outnumbered.

If the person doesn't need to be there, you may politely ask your client if the offending person could leave. Let him know that you are not comfortable with the person's behavior. If the person refuses to leave, the client wants him to stay or the offending person needs to stay, you can either reschedule for a time or place when that person won't be there, come back at another time with a co-worker or let the client know that you won't be able to work with him.

11) The client has a dangerous animal or one you can't tolerate.

If you are afraid of dogs or allergic to certain animals, you will want to be sure the client is aware of your concerns. Be sure to ask all clients if they have pets. If yes, you will need to work out acceptable solutions prior to your arrival.

If you like animals, you may not need to inquire about pets, but do be sure the pets are confined when you arrive.

> All dogs should be contained, even if the client says the dog is friendly and even if you love dogs.

Remember, you are entering that dog's territory. If an argument arises, even if it's just raised voices, the dog may decide to protect the owner.

You may also inadvertently get too close to a toy or sleeping area belonging to a protective dog. If the dog is loose, it is free to defend those items and spaces. I have seen one of my own dogs charge across two entire rooms to defend a toy (that he had been playing with hours earlier) from one of my other dogs (who was completely oblivious as to what had caused the incident.) My dogs are not the only ones who guard things they think are theirs. It is actually a very common behavior and it could put you at risk for a bite.

A big dog can accidentally cause injury by knocking you down if it puts its paws on you or leans too hard against your legs.

Small dogs may seem the most harmless, but are actually more likely to bite. Many small dogs make up for their limited bulk by having big attitudes and are not shy about using their teeth to make a point.

If you want to make contact with a dog, stay still and encourage the dog to come to you. This allows the dog to decide if it wants the attention or not and saves you from having to guess. Avoid reaching over the dog's head or petting the dog on the head as a first contact. Instead scratch under the dog's chin or the side of the dog's neck or on the dog's shoulder. Reaching over the dog's head could be seen as an aggressive move by a timid or poorly socialized dog.

Avoid staring into a dog's eyes because in dog language, that is a threat. Accepting direct eye contact is a learned behavior in dogs, it doesn't come naturally. If a dog gets frightened (reacting mode), it will revert to what comes naturally, not what has been trained (thinking mode.)

Shy dogs can pose problems too. If a dog is not confident and comfortable with having a stranger in the house, it may feel cornered or threatened simply by your presence.

Never move toward a dog that seems hesitant or afraid. When a dog is afraid, it usually has one of two reactions: fight or flight. The dog may be experiencing many of the same physical reactions that a fearful human would feel. If startled, it may react with a bite before the brain takes over and lets the dog fully analyze the situation. Because of this, you should never touch a dog that is distracted, sleeping or deaf until it chooses to come to you.

Unless you have observed, handled and trained many dogs, do not assume that you are able to read the dog's body language correctly; even people that are experts with dogs sometimes misread a dog's signals. It is safer to simply have the client confine the dog.

If you approach a house and are confronted by a loose dog, <u>stand still</u>! Look anywhere except the dog's eyes. Use your deep breathing to regain or maintain your composure. If you are carrying anything, you can keep it between you and the dog if you don't move it too fast. Most dogs will run up barking, get close enough to give you a good sniffing and then go about their business. If the dog continues to bark, very slowly take steps toward safety. If you think someone might hear, you can try yelling "Please get your dog back."

It is not recommended that you yell at a dog or act like you are going to hit the dog that continues to bark at or circle you. If the dog has been protection trained, or if the dog is very confident, these actions can cause the dog to attack. Do not continue into the dog's territory until the dog is safely confined. Even a dog that keeps its distance may feel pressured to defend its territory if you continue toward "its house."

Dog's instinct to chase and capture prey is triggered by fast movement and high pitched vocalizations. Even non-aggressive dogs can be provoked to grab a rapidly retreating object. Since they don't have hands, they use their teeth. In bite prevention courses I give to kids, they are told to stand still like a tree if approached by a loose dog or dogs. If the dog knocks them down, they are told to lie like a log (on their belly, with their hands behind their neck).

If you have a cell phone, you can call 911 and request police assistance. You could try calling the client if you think it is their dog.

Some cats can give mixed signals. They act like they want attention and then bite or scratch if you reach to pet them. Never get near any pets unless the owner is present, has given permission and has control of the pet.

If the client does not hold up his end of the bargain and has the pet(s) loose or otherwise maintained in a way you can't tolerate, then you should excuse yourself.

Most people with pets understand that not everyone loves them the way they do and they should be willing to accept that you have reservations or that you want to protect yourself. It also protects them from the liability that occurs when a pet "that is very friendly and wouldn't hurt a flea" bites or causes injury.

12) The client has a lot of distractions-- kids, projects, cooking, etc.

Some distractions are just too disruptive while others can be worked around. If the television or radio is playing at a disruptive level, you could ask the client to turn it down (or off).

If you are not able to conduct your business with the distractions, you can tell the client, "It's obvious this is not a good time for you to meet with me. Let's reschedule for a time when you will be able to devote your attention to what we need to accomplish."

If young or rowdy children are an issue (and it's not the kids that you are there to observe or help) perhaps a babysitter will need to be hired or schedule a time when the spouse can be home to watch the kids. You might be able to pick a time when the kids are in school or visiting friends.

If you arrive at the home and find the street lined with fire trucks because the neighbor's home is on fire, that might be a good time to reschedule. If you find that someone close to the client has just died or is suddenly ill or injured the client is not likely to be able to concentrate on the task at hand.

The situation or distraction may be unavoidable at that moment, but it is probable that you can reschedule for a time with less distraction.

In the case of a client with ADHD or some of the other conditions, you may have to overcome the client's propensity for distraction. I encourage you to speak with people that are more experienced in helping individuals affected by the various disorders you may encounter. This will allow you to learn more about the disorder(s) and find some helpful ways to keep the client's attention on the task or business at hand.

13) Your client is of the opposite sex and married, but you are meeting him or her without the spouse present.

In some cases this could be a perfectly normal situation. However, it could also be cause for concern. To avoid having to confront a jealous spouse, you may want to be sure the spouse is aware of the meeting. In most cases, you will have to take the word of the client. By asking, you will be bringing it to the attention of the client, who might not have considered the implications in the eyes of his or her spouse.

You could say "Will your spouse be joining us?" This allows you to inquire about marital status or learn about a "significant other" without outright asking. If he or she says "No, he/she won't be joining us," you could ask "Is he/she aware we are meeting?" In the case of spouses or family members, it usually doesn't hurt to be open and honest with clients about your feelings of unease.

You may have a client that tells you about how their spouse is the jealous type and how he or she reacted badly in a different situation. That same client may not see the conflict of your meeting without it being pointed out and addressed directly. If you have any concerns, be sure to voice them.

If you can't avoid the meeting and feel the spouse may see you as a threat, be sure to take along a friend or co-worker preferably of the same sex as the client.

14) The client or another person in the home has a medical emergency

There are several possible situations that you may not have considered that could require immediate action. For this reason, I have given them their own section of the book a bit later.

15) You are not able to help the client, but he insists that you can

This is failing to take no for an answer. Don't fall for a "compelling statement" mentioned in a previous chapter. Don't give in, just get out. The next section will give you options you can use to get out.

He may be trying to continue a "relationship" that you have shown you want to end. If you have a client that is giving other warning signals or that you are not comfortable working with you should end the association with him.

Predators and people with certain personalities do not want you to leave them. They can be controlling or clingy and are likely to try to guilt you into continuing to work with them by using compelling statements. Learn to recognize this ploy and don't fall for it.

16) You are called in to help on behalf of another person, without that person's knowledge.

Be very careful with this situation because you could be violating the law. If the person who lets you into the home does not live there, you may both be breaking trespass laws, even if he/she has a key. Never move, alter or dispose of another person's belongings without that person's consent.

Do your best to avoid entering the home if it is not the homeowner or a resident that is letting you in-- especially if you don't know whether or not the home owner has given permission for you to enter.

17) The client has exits blocked and stays between you and the only exits.

You may have cause for concern if you enter a home and see that there are bars on the windows (or you are in a living space that is higher than the second floor of the building) and you also see that other doors are blocked with piles of items or padlocked. Even if the client is not showing any signs of danger, those conditions pose a fire hazard. There should be multiple escapes from every home.

One way of keeping your exits open is though body positioning. If you watch police officers handling prisoners, you can note that they stay slightly behind them. The reason for this is that it gives them a view of the prisoner's full body. This makes tensing or other pre-flight or fight signals more apparent.

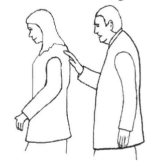

The other reason is because it is easier to control someone from behind. He or she can't see as clearly where your hands are going to strike or grab. Remember how Greg kept Jane in front of him?

> You don't want anyone behind you unless you fully trust him with your life.

Once you enter the living space and the client closes the door, motion for him to lead you rather than follow you. You can use a sweeping hand gesture and say "After you" or "Lead the way" to further encourage him to stay

in front of you. You don't want to get into the polite but comic routine that the cartoon chipmunk had with his brother:
"After you."
"Oh no no no, I insist, after you"
"I wouldn't dream of it brother, after you."

But you should do your best to insist. You could say, "I don't know your home as well as you do, so I prefer to follow" or "It is company policy that I follow, not lead."

This can also be used when moving through the house and into the various rooms. If you are in front of the client as you go through a doorway, he could close a door behind you, trapping you in a room. You should be the last to enter a room and the first to exit, and then wait outside the room for the client to get back in front of you before you move to the next room or area. If this is not your normal behavior, I suggest practicing it with family and friends until it becomes comfortable and second nature. When it becomes natural, the client with good intentions won't even notice you are doing it, but it will send a clear signal to anyone with less than desirable intentions. If he refuses to take no (as in, I don't want to lead) for an answer, raise your guard.

In a related matter, what if you enter a home and the client locks the door right after closing it? Should you be concerned? Well, that depends on the context of the situation and other signals. If the door did not need to be unlocked to let you in, the client keeps himself between you and the door and shows some of the other warning signals; you might need to start figuring out how you can get out fast.

However, if the door was locked when you arrived, then unlocked to let you in and once inside, the client acts normally, he may simply worry about security. If you're not sure, it doesn't hurt to ask "Do you have trouble with crime in this area?" If nothing else, the answer may give you more information upon which to base your feelings.

18) The living conditions in the home are hazardous or appalling

It is truly sad that in this great country of ours, some people live in deplorable conditions. In some cases mental conditions, age or disability can cause a lack of self-care or home maintenance or such a collection of items that moving though the house becomes hazardous. Insect or rodent infestations are another possibility.

Some professions see these conditions more than others. If you are likely to encounter these conditions be aware of the various hazards and how to keep yourself safe.

- Don't step anywhere that you can't see what is between your foot and the floor.

- If roaches are a visible problem, keep your feet moving to keep them from crawling up your legs.

- A medical mask may be a good idea for certain conditions to prevent the inhalation of odors or bio-contaminants.

- If the conditions warrant, calling in the health department may be the best course of action. They deal with those conditions on a regular basis and are better equipped and trained to handle them.

If conditions in the home are unsafe or unmanageable, then you may need to excuse yourself. You should be honest and let the client know that you can't help him.

You may want to suggest he contact social services for help or contact them yourself. In some cities, there are repair and clean up services available to low-income residents. Other social service departments can help with providing mental and medical treatment, meals, and extermination of pests. However incredible it may seem, there may not be others that know about the client's living conditions. Making the appropriate social services aware of the conditions may truly be the best help you can give the person.

Not all situations are that bad though. Poor lighting can be another hazard. In some cases, the client may have been living 'in the dark' for so long, he accepts it as normal. It may be that you simply need to point it out and suggest higher wattage bulbs or turning on more lights. If possible, open the window blinds to let in as much light as possible. This will make it easier and safer to work in the space.

19) You witness a crime while with the client

It could be that you witness domestic violence, animal abuse/neglect, illegal drug use, child abuse/neglect or assault. If any of these things (or other crimes) occurs in your presence, you may be required by law to report them. Get yourself out of the situation as quickly as possible and call the proper authorities. Of course you can tell the client that you won't report him if that is what you need to say to get out of the situation safely. Yes, it is a lie, but it beats the alternative which could be a client who feels you are a witness that needs to be silenced- be sure to report any threats too.

If you are with a client and you both witness a crime, such as a person getting assaulted outside the client's home or an auto accident occurs within view, you may both be witnesses. As soon as authorities are notified, both of you should separately and without discussion, write down exactly what you saw in as much detail as possible. This will make it easier to answer any questions asked by police without confusion regarding what the other witness(es) saw. Look at the suspect identification information in the *What to do after an attack* section to get as much detail as possible.

If the client doesn't want to get involved, don't let that stop you from obeying the law or being a good citizen.

20) The client shows you a weapon

This situation was worded carefully. Notice it doesn't say "client *threatens* you with a weapon." In the case of a threat you'll obviously want to get away from the client as quickly as possible. If your exits are not open or the client has physical control of you, you may have to do some quick thinking to try to talk your way free. You might also choose to submit, resist or fight. There are too many variables to tell you "If the predator does

_____, you should _____." One action does not fit all circumstances.

Keep in mind that you can change your mind about your course of action. You may at first decide that submitting is the best route and later decide you have to fight for your life.

> If you do choose to fight, remember to use surprise to your advantage, pick the best opportunity and give it everything you have. Fight for your loved ones.

If you fight half heartedly, you will only alert him to the fact that you have considered fighting and he will likely take measures to prevent further attempts. Think about the primary targets in your mind: Eyes and the throat.

The groin is a commonly used target and most likely to be protected. It won't do much good if the attacker is high on drugs or adrenalin and can't feel it. If you damage his eyes, he can't see further attacks from you and can't see your escape. If you damage his throat (it doesn't take much) then his air is disrupted and if he can't breathe, he's not likely to attempt to continue to fight. Be sure to protect your own throat too. Only you will be able to absorb the situation and determine your best course of action. Whatever the outcome, don't second-guess your actions. You can only do the best you can with the skills and knowledge you have at the time.

Once you get free and to a safe place, contact the police. I chose to word this situation as "shows you a weapon" because that is more open to context. It could range anywhere from the client pointing out an old war revolver that is framed on the wall, to having a weapon in their hand (or within reach) in a more subtlety threatening manor.

Regardless of the circumstances, if it makes you uncomfortable, let the client know and/or get yourself out of the situation. In the example of the framed weapon, if you have a serious aversion to all weapons, you may say to the client "I am not comfortable with weapons, could we get back to the subject of..." If the client apologizes and returns to a more relevant topic, I don't think there would be cause for alarm. It's likely they were just proudly pointing out a valued possession.

If you feel it is a veiled threat, get out of the situation as fast as you can. If you simply turn and run, unless you are right next to an exit door that opens onto a well traveled street, you have let him know that you are terrified and a good victim. He may be able to catch you before you get outside.

Giving an excuse from the next section would be preferred while continuing to play the part of a confident woman. Do your best to not show fear even though you may be terrified inside. He is likely using the veiled threat as a test to see your reaction and determine your suitability as his next victim. If you fall apart and show that you are terrified, he knows you are probably an easy and cooperative victim. If instead, you remain confident (or appear to be confident) he is much more likely to think twice about continuing any attack. He won't know if you are confident because you know martial arts or if you have a weapon as well but confidence implies that you can handle yourself.

Predators don't want victims that are still in their thinking, rational mind because those are dangerous. They want them in the reactionary fight or flight mindset because many women tend to submit rather than fight when terrified.

About the possible situations:
I hope that you have found the above situations thought provoking and helpful, without having them be too frightening. I'm sure I could list many more, but my intent was to show some of the possibilities to make you more aware and to induce some thought about your safety and how you can increase it. Also to let you know you have the ability to affect how others see you-- don't be a good victim. Learn all that you can to gain the type of confidence that radiates. Even if you feel frightened or unsure of yourself, practice taking on the persona of a confident woman.

How to get out

In this section, I'm going to give you more to ponder and learn. Many of the above scenarios called for getting out of the client's space/home, but didn't go into the specifics of how that could be done. That is what this section will cover; along with some general tips and preparations you can use to help you get out if the situation arises.

If you are not comfortable, you don't have to stay- Don't think that you have to hear the client out, or wait for his response to a statement you make or get permission from him before you leave. If your instincts are telling you to get out, DO IT-- NOW. It is up to you whether you want to use an excuse that allows you to still have a working relationship with the client or if you don't care that your excuse might be perceived as rude and unprofessional. Your life may be at stake, being considered rude should not even be a concern.

Cell phones
These have proven time and again that they can be real lifesavers in many different situations.

> I highly recommend that you have a cell phone, keep the power on and keep it <u>with</u> you when you are with a client.

If you're worried that an incoming call could be a distraction, put it on vibrate and don't answer it. By keeping it on you at all times, you keep it accessible and it can help you create an exit. If you were to leave it in your bag on the main floor and all looks safe till the client gets you in the basement, you may not have an opportunity to get to your phone.

Have a Signal
Simply following the advice above may not be enough for some situations. You should work out a signal with a friend, family member or co-worker in case of an emergency where you don't want to let on to the client that you know or think you are in trouble.

If you keep your phone on you, then you are always able to say "Oh, my phone is vibrating, let me get this call." You could then press a pre-programmed speed dial button to call your friend while you act like you are talking to the "caller." Or you could say you missed the call, but were expecting an important call from your office so you need to call in or they will worry. Another option is to say that the person who just called wouldn't call unless it was very important, so you need to call them back.

Once you get your buddy on the phone, you can work the pre-arranged signal into your conversation with him or her.

> A signal like; "Oh no! When?!" can give you an excuse to leave.

Your signal to a friend should be worked out in advance to determine what you want him or her to do when he or she hears you give the signal. It would be for serious emergencies, so don't let your friend take it lightly and don't over use it.

One possibility would be for the friend to call the police and send them to your location if you don't call back in three minutes. By allowing three minutes, you give yourself the time to see if your "Oh my, when did that happen" can help get you out of the house without the assistance of law enforcement.

After you give the signal, you could tell the client, "There's been an emergency! I have to go." You don't have to give him an explanation, just head for the door. You can tell him you can't discuss it and that you have to go because it is really serious.

If you are able to get out, call your friend back when you are safe. Three to five minutes should be plenty of time. If the client does not let you leave, you know the police will be sent. Just stay as calm and rational as possible.

If you get out well after you know your friend has notified the police, get a safe distance away and call 911 to explain what happened. The police officers will likely need you to meet with them so that it can be verified that you are okay.

> When your friend calls the police, be sure he or she stresses that it was a pre-arranged signal of danger and that if the officers don't make contact with you, to assume it is a hostage situation.

Of course this won't work if your contact doesn't answer the phone. Be sure that whomever you have chosen as your contact will be available to answer a call from you.

If she understands why she is important to your safety she will be less likely to leave the house "just for a moment to get the mail" or get so wrapped up in a television program that she doesn't answer the phone.

If your contact is at work, be sure that you work out an alternative in advance in case she is on another phone call or with her own client. You can say, "The phone is busy, let me try her other number" and either use a different number for the same person or try a different contact.

Keep in mind that if you use the client's phone to make a phone call, he may be able to use the special phone company features to see the number you dialed. Never call home or a friend or another client from a client's phone.

Know the address
All of the above steps could fail miserably if you and/or your buddy don't know where you are! It sounds simple enough, but do you memorize the address of your client?

I have trouble recalling numbers, but can usually recall the street name. What I do, is write the address numbers on a tiny slip of paper and put it under the clear pouch of my cell phone case. You could do that with the whole address too.

Another option is to write it on a piece of paper you put in your pocket. That way, if the attacker takes your cell phone, you can still tell police where you are if you are able to get to another phone.

The written list works best if you have multiple clients to see in one day. Just cross them off as you see each one so it's clear in an emergency which address you are visiting.

If client confidentiality is an issue, put the client's information in a sealed envelope and give it to your buddy who only opens it if the signal is given. If you have several client meetings in one day, make a list of them in the order you plan to visit and seal that in an envelope.

It will be helpful to your friend if you call in before each client to say "I'm about to enter Gary's home" or you could just say "client number three's home." The person you call would only have that person's information in the event of an emergency. It is always a good idea to have at least one other person know exactly where you will be.

Precious minutes can be lost if the information has to be deciphered from a meeting planner or calendar of appointments.

If you work out of an office then policies and procedures should be put in place so that all field employees have a way to call in and let a central organizer know where they are and where they are going next. If someone asks where you are, there should always be a designated person in the office that knows. Create some type of a system for that person to keep track of everyone in a way that would alert him or her to delays or discrepancies.

Keeping Track

Offices get busy and your contact might lose track of who has called in and who hasn't. I suggest a separate labeled timer for each field worker. When the employee calls in, the timer starts. When the field worker is finished with a location, the timer is turned off till the next client's home. If a timer goes off before the employee calls in, then that person gets a phone call from the office to check on them. By using timers, the employee can give an estimate of the amount of time he or she plans to be with the client when the "I'm on location" call is made. If they are uneasy about a location, the timer could be set for 10 minutes so that a "check-up" call is made to her fairly quickly. No employee should be out of contact for over an hour, so one-hour timers should work nicely. Phone numbers for each location should be included on the visit list in case the location is out of cell range or in a "dead spot." If the employee doesn't answer their cell phone, the client's home should be called.

If each timer has a cover, then it is obvious with just a glance, who is still in the field at the end of the day. At the end of each day, all the timers should have their covers on. At the start of the next day, as each employee turns in their route list with the addresses she is visiting and heads out the door, their timer is uncovered. When they check-in at their first stop, their timer starts.

If you get into trouble and can't get to your phone (or you are in an area without good reception) your contact may be the only person that notices that you haven't checked in. If you are injured you will want to be missed as soon as possible and not have to wait till the end of the day before someone notices you haven't checked in for the past few hours. If the police know where to start looking for you, it will help in the event that you are abducted or kidnapped. If your contact only knows that you were working "on the north side of town" today the police won't even know where to start their search. If you were to lose control of your car and drive off the road into a deep ravine, would anyone notice you were missing or know where to look? They should.

Having a system in place like the one above will make it easier to show the police that employees HAVE to check-in. When you don't, it helps show that foul play is possible. Without some indication of foul play, police usually require that 24 hours has passed before an adult can be reported as missing. More information on that is in the "*Abduction Avoidance*" section.

The excuses

Before you go into your next client's home, you should come up with (and practice saying) a few excuses. You need to practice them, because many people are terrible liars. You have to be able to say it in such a way that you almost believe it.

> In fact, if you let yourself believe your excuse, you will be able to deliver it more convincingly.

I have listed a few to get you thinking of possibilities, but I suggest you come up with some of your own that feel natural for you to say.

There are a few simple rules that your excuses should follow. First, you can't use an excuse for which the client could provide a solution. An example of an excuse to avoid would be "I have a headache so I need to end the meeting early." The client could offer you over the counter pain medication (or what *looks* like over the counter pain medication.)

Secondly, it has to be something that you can say convincingly. Don't make an excuse about your kids if you don't have kids. There is a surprising amount of information available on the Internet that people with ill intentions could find if they know where to look. There is also the possibility that the "client" has been watching you. He might already know you don't have kids. Keep the excuses believable and irrefutable.

Good Excuses:

- "I have a medical condition that is acting up and I need my prescription". If they ask you the condition, you can say, "I'd rather not discuss it."

- "There's been an emergency, I have to go" after a fake or real phone call.

- "Now that I see the situation, I realize I'm not going to be able to help you, let me see if I can get you a reference of someone who can." If they resist, they are refusing to take 'no' for an answer-- leave.

- "I just remembered I forgot to cancel another appointment that begins in just a few minutes. I'm going to have to cut this meeting short." If they don't accept the meeting being cut short say, "Well, let me call my office so they can let my next client know I'll be a bit late," then use the emergency signal.

If you can leave after hearing of the "emergency", very well; if not, you know it's not a false alarm being given to your buddy.

If the client meets you outside and you have not yet entered the home, you can say you forgot something at the office that you have to take care of or need to get. Some of the above excuses will also work. Be sure you don't enter into any home where your instincts are telling you there is danger.

If you haven't arrived at the home, but find the neighborhood is one you don't want to work in alone, you can say your car broke down or you got sick. That gives you some time to find some help to accompany you when you go back. If you know you will not go back, it is best to let the client know "something has come up" and you will not be able to help him.

Protecting Yourself From Violence During Home Visits by Chris Puls

Plans and preparations

> Proper prior planning prevents poor
> *(Self)* protection practices

The following are additional things you can do or consider. Many are things to do prior to meeting with the client to increase your level of safety or awareness.

Safety in numbers
Take another person with you if at all possible. There really IS more safety in numbers. If things get out of hand, the more help you have, the more likely you will be to get out safely. It is much less common for attacks to occur when there is more than one person as the potential victim. Predators need PC—Privacy and Control. By having another person with you, it eliminates privacy. It can also help you if he tries for control.

You constantly evaluate both privacy and control because your instincts know they can be dangerous. Now you need to make the decision to listen when your instincts point out PC situations.

If you have reservations about meeting a client alone, but you don't have a co-worker to take with you, you can have a friend or family member drive you to your appointment. If the client notices, you can tell him your car broke down. If he doesn't notice, be sure to casually point out that you have help waiting for you. You can say, "My car broke down, but my friend was available to give me a ride." If you have nothing to fear from the client, he will likely be impressed that you went to "such trouble" to keep the appointment. If he had ill intentions, seeing that you have back up waiting just outside could save you from an attack. It lets him know that someone else knows where you are and can help you or call for help if he goes though with his plans. I don't recommend having your ride drop you off however, because that leaves you stranded in the event of an emergency.

Violent Visitors
Would you know if your client was having trouble with an ex-husband, old boyfriend, a stalker or a teen on drugs? Depending on the work you do, you might. If you had access to public records, you might find a restraining order if one was filed or criminal records if you had information on the aggressor. But in most cases you wouldn't know unless the client told you.

Some work puts you at extra risk. Jobs like social services, child welfare and elder care. Animal control officers can also be at risk. When you have the authority to remove family members or pets from someone's care, the possibility for violence can get very high.

The best course of action if you know a hostile situation is likely, would be to have your meeting in a location other than the home if possible. In the home, the aggressors have the advantage of familiarity and knowledge of the locations of possible weapons. If you meet instead at a more public place or your office you can start on equal or more comfortable ground for you.

If you have to work in a situation where you think there is a possibility that another person could arrive and interfere, you will want to have at least one other person with you that can wait outside. They will be an early warning signal for you. Be sure that he or she doesn't park in such a way that the car can get blocked in. It may be helpful if the car is parked in such a way that it allows your helper to watch the house and road without being obvious which house you are in. If they see the troublemaker arrive, they can blow the car horn and/or call you or the police. I would advise that you call the police before you arrive to let them know of the situation (if they don't already know) so that if you call, they will arrive quickly. There is the possibility that if the police are not busy, they could send a car to the location or have a car patrol in that area.

Make sure at least one person knows where you are going for each visit you make and be sure to contact that person after the visit so he or she knows you are safe. Also let your contact know what to do if you don't call by a certain time. If you change the itinerary of your visits, be sure to notify your contact of the new schedule.

> By getting into this habit it will make it easier on you because you won't have to think about calling in, it will just be "second nature." Your contact will be more likely to notice if you break the habit.

Having a contact that can tell police "She ALWAYS calls, and now we haven't heard from her" is more powerful than, "She said she would call, but sometimes she forgets." The police will ask if you have forgotten to call in the past. It is up to you to be sure that the person contacting the police for you can say, "No, she always calls."

Auto safety
Avoid trying shortcuts you don't know well. They could cause you to become lost.

Be sure your vehicle is in good working order and has at least half a tank of fuel. You don't want to be stranded on the side of the road. If this should happen, lock your doors and don't open them for anyone. You should have a cell phone on you to call for help. If not, tell anyone that stops to please send the police. Only roll down the window one inch. If you have a window that rolls down all the way electronically and automatically when you press the button then practice stopping it. If your windows don't work with the car turned off, then yell through the closed window.

> SEND POLICE

Buy or create a large sign that says "SEND POLICE." Be sure to have one in each car and post it immediately if you find yourself stranded. There are predators that cruise the highways looking for opportunities. If they know everyone going by has possibly been calling the police, it makes you a much less appealing target because the predator won't know when the police might arrive. The people that are not predators are more willing to make a call for you than to stop to help anyway. It's okay if the police dispatch gets multiple calls about your car. Multiple calls may even help speed the response time of the police. The signs are available at: http://www.surviveInstitute.com/ under the products link. Some great books and videos are also available there.

It is extra important to have a well-serviced vehicle and a cell phone when the temperatures start to rise. If it is ninety degrees outside and your car won't start, you won't be able to remain in the safety of a closed car. If at all possible, try to get the car into a shaded area. If you are outside of your vehicle and you feel a "Good Samaritan" is actually a wolf in disguise, you have a few options.

You can keep the car between you and the stranger or get under the car. When the stranger sees that you are trying to remain on the other side of the car, he will probably react in one of two ways. He could get frustrated and try a stronger pursuit (such as over the car) or he could back off and apologize for scaring you. The second option is most likely the reaction of a harmless stranger, but don't let it cause you to drop your guard. It could just as easily be a ploy by a thinking predator trying to win your trust.

If you get under the car you will have plenty of things to grab onto and can make yourself a very difficult target. Please be sure you have your keys with you! You don't want the predator to figure out how to get your car running with you under it.

Under your car won't be a pleasant place to be, but it sure beats the alternative possibility of being dragged off or raped in your back seat. Be aware that if your car was running recently, some things under the car may be very hot. The next time you take your car in for service and it is up on the lift, ask the mechanic to point out the places that get hot so you can avoid grabbing them if you have to retreat under your car in an emergency.

By wedging yourself under the car you make yourself a very difficult target and a predator is likely to abandon his plans and look for an easier target.

Any weapon you may have should be kept in your hand the entire time you are stranded. Even an ink pen can make a formidable weapon if stabbed into a hand that is trying to grab you (or any soft body part such as the eyes, throat or groin).

Keep all weather and emergency gear in your vehicle. If you have an accident or a break down in cold weather, you will be very glad you packed a blanket, gloves and a warm hat.

Create an emergency duffle bag. This will hold your emergency gear and is easily transported from car to car. Items like bottled water, a first aid kit, a light weight jump suit or long T-shirt, flares, "send police" sign, blanket, gloves, hat, and spare pair of shoes.

If you know how to change a tire and think you might do that if the situation arises, keep a pair of lightweight overalls in your emergency duffle bag. The overalls will protect your clothes from dirt and grease. If you are likely to be wearing a skirt, a long oversized T-shirt may be a better option because a skirt would bunch up inside overalls. A spare pair of athletic shoes will be easier to work in than high heels, if you still choose to wear high heels.

Emergency flares are a good idea because they make your car more visible if it is after dark and not well lit in the area where you have to stop.

A lit flare can also make a formidable weapon because of the molten content that can be sent flying with just a flick of the wrist. I know that for a fact. While setting flares for an auto accident, I burned a hole in the top of a thick leather shoe when some accidentally dripped on my foot.

The two-inch flame shooting out of the end is a good deterrent too! Most are easy to light and work on the same principle as a match. Be sure to read and understand the directions before you need to use them. Keep the flare pointed away from you as you light it and after it is lit. Do your best not to breathe the vapors and smoke from the flares. The smoke has a strong sulfur or acidic smell. Bend the flexible wires on each side down to form a base for the flare to rest upon. The lit end of the flare should be pointed at an angle toward the sky and facing approaching traffic. Flares are available at most auto parts stores along with reflectors that are easier to use, but don't serve as emergency weapons.

You can still drive slowly on a flat tire for a short distance. It is better to take a chance of damaging the tire rim, than to get stranded in an unsafe location.

Lock your car doors as you get in! This one tip could save many people from car jacking, abduction and robbery if it was heeded. This is especially important if all of your doors open by remote at the same time. Locks are very simple prevention tools, but they only work if they are used. Try to minimize the amount of time that doors are unlocked between when you approach and enter your vehicle and the time you get inside. Your hand is automatically near the door lock button when you pull the door closed, so make it a habit to hit the lock button as you pull the door closed. As a temporary reminder until the habit is formed, write "locks" on a small Post-it note and stick it to the center of your steering wheel or at the bottom of the display (speedometer) panel where it's easily visible but not blocking your view of any of the gauges.

Don't let yourself get distracted as you approach and enter you vehicle. Stay aware of your surroundings. Be sure your keys are in your hand as you approach your car so that you can get in quickly without having to take your attention from the area around you.

> Please don't stand by your car digging in your purse!

Get in the habit of locking your doors as soon as you get in. Once this becomes habit, you won't have to make a conscious effort to effect this excellent safety tool, it will just happen automatically. Some cars now have this feature built in and all the doors lock when the car is put in gear or it reaches a certain speed. This is nice, but it happens too late to protect you from a predator that just saw you get into your car with a big heavy purse or an expensive package.

If you are a home care nurse, you will want to be extra cautious because robbers and thieves may target you thinking you have drugs to steal.

Watch for anyone hanging out in the area of your car and don't approach until they leave. Once you get to your car, get in quickly and lock your doors.

Know how to get to your destination so you don't have to stop to ask for directions or try to look at a map while driving. If you are not sure of the location, get clear directions and find the location on a map before you leave. Have the map and directions easily accessible along with a call back number in case you get lost.

If you need to make a call (or answer one) on your cell phone while driving, pull over at the next available safe location to talk. Stay aware of your surroundings while on the phone and keep your doors locked. It may be a good idea to keep the car running and in gear so that if someone does approach the car in a threatening manner you can leave quickly.

> Would you know what to do if someone came to your car window and pointed a gun at you making a demand? If your car is in gear, you should stomp on the accelerator and get out of the situation fast. If it's not in gear and your doors are locked, "faint" onto the horn.

Acting like you have fainted can be useful if you are in an area with lots of people or in a locked car. A predator is looking for a cooperative victim not a seemingly unconscious one. If you are attacked outside your car you could tell the attacker you won't resist and then act as though you have fainted. Lying in a heap on the ground, you are more likely to get helpful attention than if you fight with an attacker. I don't recommend trying this unless there are plenty of bystanders that are likely to notice you. If no one is around, the predator may try to drag you away. Read more about this technique in the *avoiding abduction* chapter.

Bystanders are more willing to help if they think you might be having a medical emergency than if it looks like you are being attacked. But don't rely on others to save you. Keep this trick in your arsenal and use it if you feel it can get you the attention you need or to convince the attacker you are not an easy victim.

Keep items of value out of site in your vehicle's trunk or in a covered, unmarked bin. This will lessen the risk of a break in to your vehicle while you are visiting. It can also prevent a "smash and grab" robbery. This is when a robber waits for you to stop at a traffic light or stop sign, smashes your window and grabs your purse or other visible valuables and runs before you even realize what has happened.

Limit the amount of cash and credit cards you carry. If you feel you need to take them with you, have them locked in your car, out of sight during the visit. Put them out of site before you arrive at the client's home. This will prevent onlookers from seeing you place your purse or other valuables into the trunk. If you place valuables in your trunk while in a public place, watch for anyone that might be following you when you leave the area. If you only drive a short distance away and a thief has followed you then he knows you have something worth stealing behind the backseat. Trunk spaces are accessible in most cases because many car models have back seats that fold down or pull out. Thieves know that if they break a window, they can open a door and get to the back seat quickly.

Even if witnesses are present, it is unlikely that anyone will prevent or stop the crime. The best you can hope for is a decent description if the witness stays around long enough to report it to you or the police. Unfortunately most people would just shake their heads at the criminal activity and go on their way (If they even noticed it as criminal activity.)

If you have a pick up truck you may want to consider a lockbox that fits inside the bed of the truck just behind the cab. These are typically used for tools but work well as a makeshift trunk. Be sure the box is attached to the body of the truck to keep it from being lifted out.

In a van or SUV, the best you can do is to keep valuables out of site in an unmarked bin or box. Regardless of your vehicle type, don't use a coat or blanket to cover valuables. A lumpy coat or blanket is an invitation to thieves because they figure, "if it wasn't important or valuable, it wouldn't have been covered."

Keep CD's and loose change out of site as well since these are primary targets of juvenile offenders. The  child thief may not take any items of great value to you during his crime but he will break a window that can be costly to replace and the mental toll of being a crime victim can be more costly.

Avoid parking near vans or trucks. They can hide an assailant and provide a means of concealing you if you are pulled inside. Just because a vehicle is in the client's driveway doesn't mean it belongs to the client.

Don't park in the driveway. It is too easy to get blocked in especially in the case of a realtor that has a client following in his own car. If parking areas are not available park on the street or across the end of the driveway. Pull into parking spots in parking lots instead of backing into them. If someone does try to block you in, you can use the power of your engine to push and ram them out of the way using the back of your car. If you tried to use the front of your car for the same purpose, there is a greater chance of damage to the engine which would disable the car.

Try to park in well-lit areas and avoid isolated areas. This will help protect the vehicle and its contents, as well as making it safer for you to return to your vehicle. If you arrive in daylight, but will be leaving after dark, look for available light sources (utility lights, security lights, etc.) and park near those if possible.

Lock all the doors and close all the windows even if it is hot. It only takes a small crack to allow an amateur thief access to your door controls with a homemade device. It takes an accomplished car thief about 15 seconds from the time he approaches your car to the time he drives off. This includes using a tool to get the door locks to open (about 4 seconds) and breaking the steering column or using some means to "hot wire" the car.

Thankfully the car makers are always coming up with ways to make this process more difficult for thieves. **Unfortunately, this has caused the crime of carjacking.** The thieves are finding it easier to steal an occupied car, than to get into an unoccupied one. With the addition of car locator devices like LoJack, the thieves know they have a bigger window of time to get away if they have the owner with them. If they dump the person in a very remote area (or harm them), it gives them even more time before the owner can report the car stolen.

Betty is a realtor who at times feels like her car is her office. She does a lot of driving. So it's not surprising that she has seen her share of auto related incidents and crimes. You can learn from her mistakes.

The scariest crime occurred on a crisp fall day when she was driving her brand new Cadillac in a semi rural area. There was a car in front of her and a car behind her. Around them at the moment were farm fields that were recently cleared of their crops. When the car in front of her was stopped at a stop sign, Betty pulled up behind it as she normally would. That's when the passenger from the car behind her got out and ran up to her door. He was wearing a ski mask and Betty's first thought was to drive around the car in front of her. But she had pulled too close. She blew the horn, but the car in front wasn't moving.

While this was going on, the man at her door shattered the window, opened the door, and with a gun he ordered Betty to get out.

As soon as she was out, that's when the car in front of Betty's decided to move. It registered to her that the driver in front was an accomplice just as the driver behind. Before she could think, they were gone.

She was left standing in the middle of the road with no money, no cell phone and without a clear idea of where, exactly, she was. Betty was lucky that day. All the thieves wanted was her car. It could have been much worse. So what did Betty learn from this?

When you stop behind another vehicle, be sure to stop far enough back that you can see where the

back tires of that vehicle touch the road. This assures that you'll have enough room to get around it if you need to do so. Also, keep your cell phone ON you.

If she had done this, then her first reaction of driving around the car in front of her would have been possible.

> Criminals rely on you to panic and freeze.

As you wait for the light to change or the traffic to move, play through some what-if's in your head. **Develop a plan of action so you can be ready**. You can be just as clever as a criminal. Take a moment to imagine some of the ways a criminal could try to get what he wants from you. Then go a step farther and think of ways that you know you could implement to foil his plans. By looking at things through the eyes of a criminal, you can then develop the automatic awareness to protect yourself.

When leaving the client's home- Have your keys ready as you approach your car and check the interior for anyone hiding inside before you get in. As soon as you are inside, lock the doors and don't sit there working on anything that takes your attention from your surroundings.

Clothing
Although I don't recommend wearing high heels; Women who wear them should keep a change of shoes with them in case a heel breaks.

Can you run in your shoes? Can you get them off easily so you can run without them if you need to? Many women's shoes are designed for looks, not speed. What about that skin tight skirt? Keep this in mind when selecting your outfit for client meetings. It is possible to be very professional and classy, while maintaining your ability to move quickly. Find outfits with pockets that can hold a cell phone, your ID and your keys when you select business clothes.

Don't remove your shoes if it's not an emergency. Bare feet are much more prone to injury from objects on or in the floor. They are also more vulnerable to being stomped on to incapacitate you.

Don't wear expensive jewelry that could entice a robber on your way to or from the visit, particularly in less appealing areas of town.

Carry a briefcase instead of a purse. A purse is always associated with money by thieves and robbers. They are less likely to target a briefcase or attaché case that they assume is holding papers that are worthless to them. However, avoid cases that look like they might contain a lap top since those are high on the list of items targeted by thieves.

Food and Drinks
Never accept food or drinks from the client- It may seem like you are being impolite, but many women have been drugged before they suspected anything was wrong with the client or the situation. If you can't wait till after the session, take a bottled drink with you and keep track of who gets near it. I don't recommend open cups that allow easy access to the liquid. It is best to wait till the end of the meeting to quench your thirst or satisfy your appetite. It's not worth the risk.

Rohypnol is a tasteless, odorless drug that dissolves completely in liquid. When ingested, it incapacitates for hours and erases memories of anything that happened while the drug was in the system. It causes physical effects that make it look as though the victim is drunk. Typical feeling after ingestion is dizzy and disoriented. This allows someone to add it to a drink in a public place, and then look like a Good Samaritan by helping the "drunken" woman to a car. There are other drugs that work in a similar way so don't take a chance.

If food or drink is offered, all you need to say is "No thank you." You don't need to get any more elaborate than that. If you try to make excuses like "I'm on a diet" or "I only drink 'x' type of drink," the client may be able to produce something that is not restricted by your excuse.

Try not to plan meetings at meal times or in ways where the client might feel compelled to provide food. If you are eating a meal with someone you don't know well and fully trust, don't leave any food or drink that you plan to come back and consume.

Couples and women are not always safe- Most people figure that it is only single men they need to watch. While statistically, these are the most common assailants, it is not unheard of for predators to be female and/or to work with a partner.

One couple that would tell young ladies they had a future in modeling formed such a partnership. The presence of the woman at the meetings put the "models" at ease. Sadly, the woman was part of the scheme to drug the ladies (using the availability of open drinking glasses in a restaurant) and then photograph them in ways they never intended to be photographed. The drug they used (most likely Rohypnol) caused the women to appear intoxicated and made them easy to escort out of the restaurant. It also caused memory impairment and left them unsure if anything had happened. Because of this, the pair was able to affect the lives of many women before getting caught.

Hot drink as a weapon- If the client is drinking a hot beverage it could be used as a weapon by splashing it into your face. But it works both ways. You could just as easily use it against him if you needed to.

Leave your stuff

> If things get out of control and you feel you are in danger, don't stop to collect your things.

Things can be replaced or can be retrieved when you get help. Your life is much more important than your stuff. Just get out! Keep your car and house keys on you (or at least spares) so that if you do have to leave your stuff, you can still get in your car and leave. If you have to leave your stuff and it includes keys, be sure to change any locks associated with those keys even if you recover them later. There are several methods of making impressions or copies of keys that can be used to make duplicates later.

If a client has made you frightened enough to leave his house without your things, you probably don't want him to show up at your house with the keys (or copies) to get inside.

It's a good idea to only have one client file in your bag at a time. If you have to leave your stuff, you won't be leaving behind the files of other clients. You might not want to put derogatory notes about your clients on any papers that might end up in their home. If they see the comments, it could possibly create a very uncomfortable and embarrassing situation.

Protect your personal information
Do not give clients your home address or home phone number. Even if you work from home get a voice pager or even better, a cell phone. Instead of using your home address, rent a P.O. Box. It is cheap insurance that makes it more difficult for someone to find where you live.

Female employees should not give their real last name or have it on any nametags. Having your last name available makes it too easy for others to find your address and personal information.

Anyone with knowledge of the Internet can find more information about you than you may have thought possible. You could even use a different last name at work to protect yourself from unwanted visitors at your home. Just make sure your co-workers and boss are aware of the name you choose so they don't give away your real name. As long as you explain the reason behind the "name change," it shouldn't cause too much concern.

Your paychecks will still have your real name on them and you won't be using the fake name on legal documents. If the client discovers your real name later, you can explain that the fake name is for security purposes or is a "maiden name."

If you have a business website, be sure it is not registered to your home address. The address used for registration is easily available to folks that know about the tools that divulge that public information.

If you are a realtor-
Don't ever hold an open house by yourself. Open house signs are like neon billboards that predators can use to find women alone. If you think about it from the predator's perspective, the odds of finding a woman alone are high, neighbors won't notice people going in and out, there are fingerprints all over the house from strangers and the realtor probably doesn't know that home as well as she might know her own. There is also a very good chance that there are no weapons in the home for the realtor to use to protect herself, especially if the house is vacant. The signs and advertisements make it very easy for predators to find you so you need

to be extra cautious. I recommend always having a partner with you. Of course this has not prevented attacks by armed predators. So you also want to be sure someone is calling in to check on you regularly. Or it would be wise to call in to a buddy or coworker on a regular basis during the showing. If you don't call, be sure someone checks on you. If you have a bad feeling about someone, use the pre-arranged signal with your office.

Say you'll need to close the house and leave after you hear of the "emergency." It is better to lose a possible sale than to lose your life.

In Cincinnati, two realtors were showing an open house in an upscale neighborhood. They kept the front door locked, but opened it for people that rang the doorbell. When the predator rang the doorbell, he looked harmless so the women opened the door. As soon as he was inside, he pulled a gun, locked the front door and attacked the women. The women were robbed, assaulted and left tied up in the house. A neighbor walking his dog heard the women yelling for help several hours after the attack.

This predator was caught. One of the women bit his hand and when he tried to pawn their jewelry, just hours after the attack, the pawn shop clerk noticed that he was trying to hide his hand. Police tracked him down because he used his real address at the pawn shop! It is thought that this predator was responsible for multiple attacks in the area. This includes an attack on a clerk in a shoe store in a neighboring state. That attack occurred during business hours.

Avoid using a "glamour shot" in your advertisements. Predators have been known to "victim shop" in realty magazines or other trade papers using the photos.

General tips
Try to schedule home visits only during daylight hours. Daylight will help you see street signs and house numbers so you don't get lost. It also creates less hiding places for assailants. Hazards like ice or broken porch steps will be more visible as well. If you are going into a less than desirable neighborhood, plan your visit for the morning hours when most of the night time criminal element is asleep. Be aware, however, that home break-in's often occur during the day because less people are at home. This means more vacant homes for them and fewer witnesses. It also means that less people might be around to help or hear you if trouble occurs.

In the case of a sudden downpour, **an umbrella can help you present a proper appearance**, rather than arriving at the door soaking wet. It can also alleviate the need to run on wet surfaces.

In the case of abduction (more on this topic in the next section), an attacker may use a weapon to convince you to go with them voluntarily. If you say you will cooperate and then "faint," the attacker now has to either drag or carry you (which would cause unwanted attention) or abandon his plans. Anyone that has tried to pick up a toddler than has gone limp in protest knows how hard it can be. Imagine trying to pick up an adult that has done the same thing. Of course this only works if there are witnesses close by.

At home, leave a list of the credit cards you have, their card numbers and expiration dates. You'll also need the contact numbers that are usually listed on the back of the cards. By having this list, if any card gets stolen, you will have the vital information you need to cancel the account as quickly as possible. Be sure you update the list when you get a new card.

If there are people or conditions outside the client's home, such as loose dogs or a group of rowdy teens that makes you nervous, call the client and have him or her meet you outside before you exit your vehicle.

Leave something by the entry door. This trick was mentioned before, but I'll mention it again. You plan for the worst and hope for the best. Of course, the better your planning and practice, the more likely the visit will be good.

> Leaving an item by the front door gives you an excuse to get near that exit.

It can be your coat, a bag or a briefcase. Possibly even a bag of stuff you don't really need, but that doesn't look out of place when you bring it in and set it just inside the door. Keep a lip balm, gum or mints in it. If things get uneasy, it gives you the option of going to the door but allows you to return to the client if it was a false alarm.

Avoid the kitchen if you can. There are many potential weapons there such as knives, pots/pans, boiling water, hot stove, etc.)

There are no laws of nature that say women can't attack women (or men). Is it less likely? Sure. Just be aware that it is possible so you don't give yourself a false sense of security or an excuse to ignore your instinct.

Do not sit if the client is standing. Sitting puts you at a disadvantage because the standing client can maneuver much more quickly. The chair could also be used to "pin" you in place.

When selecting a seat at a table, choose the seat that allows you to keep your back to a wall instead of a doorway or large open space. You don't want to give any accomplices the opportunity to sneak up behind you. Many police officers get in the habit of selecting the chair with the best view of the door or room and do it even when off duty. The table can be pushed or kicked out of the way in an emergency and the wall at your back acts in your favor when you use it as leverage to push against while fending off an attack. Avoid sitting in a corner where an attacker could trap you. As you perfect your people watching skills, see if you can pick out possible off duty law enforcement in restaurants and other public places.

Stress relief- Client visits can be very stressful. Be sure to include relaxation time in your schedule. Stretching and/or exercising can help combat the effects of stress. There are many ways to relieve stress and you should be looking out for your health by taking advantage of them.

Protecting Yourself From Violence During Home Visits by Chris Puls

Abduction Avoidance

If you search the Internet, you can find lots of info about teaching kids to be safe from abductors. Unfortunately, there is very little information available for adults.

> You may think that adult abduction is not a common problem because you don't hear about it on the news, but sadly it is more common than you might think. Most adult abductions are classified as "Missing Person" reports.

Unless factors of criminal activity can be shown or "foul play" is suspected, many police departments require a 24-hour period to elapse before a report on a missing adult can be made! This is why it is critical that you get into the habit of letting people know where you are and where you are going. If you break from that habit, it can help the reporting person convince the police of possible foul play. If you occasionally forget to call in, it will be less likely for your contact and the police to take a missed call seriously.

Do whatever you need to do to get yourself into the habit of calling in to someone. The reason for the twenty-four hour waiting period is because several "missing person" reports are for people that have had disputes with family or friends and just "took a walk" or have made a decision to stay away from the person that reports them missing.

However, that is not always the case. It is usually the victims that are not found, or the ones that are found dead, that make the news. Often, in those cases, the first crime committed was abduction.

The most common abductor is a white male in his twenties or thirties, but he could range in age from a young teen to an older man. Don't rule out the possibility based only on his age or race. He will likely be dressed in a way that helps him blend in with others in the area. This means that he could be well dressed or he may be dressed more casually depending on the situation.

Abductors generally have two motives-rape or other violence. Almost all are looking to forcefully dominate someone; usually this involves sexual acts or torture.

How they get you where they want you can also vary depending on the situation. It may be a violent surprise attack or a cunning lure. A third motive, though much less common in the United States, is money-- holding you for ransom.

The best way to combat the sudden violent attack is to keep yourself out of vulnerable situations. Be aware of your surroundings and try to have others with you. When walking to your car from a mall or shopping center, wait till others walk out to their cars. If you can, have your client walk you to your car or at least watch from a window to be sure you get in your car safely. Avoid places that are secluded or dark. Keep your guard up and be aware of your surroundings as you approach and leave the client's home. Avoid looking nervous or like a secret service agent, just use a casual look around.

> Something as simple as being asked what time it is can cause you to look down at your watch and take your eyes off of a predator. This makes you vulnerable to a surprise attack.

Instead of looking down at your watch, raise your wrist to eye level. This does two things; it allows you to see both your watch and the person asking for the time. It also puts your arm up which can be used to block an attack.

If you are walking or jogging along a street, face the traffic. This will allow you to see who is approaching and prevents someone from driving up behind you where you may not see him till it is too late.

To avoid being a victim of the cunning lure, trust your instincts. These predators tend to play upon our desire to help. They may fake an injury, ask you to help a sick friend or act lost. If he says he needs help, tell him you will find someone to help him and walk or run away toward the nearest people. If he tells you about an emergency, tell him you will call 911 and then leave him to go for help even if you have a cell phone on you.

If someone stops near you to ask for directions, stay away from his vehicle. If he causes your guard to rise, turn and walk away from his direction of travel and get to the nearest place with people as quickly as possible. If he puts the vehicle in reverse to follow you-- run!

If your job puts you at risk for kidnapping (holding you for ransom) your employer should have guidelines and safety training available for you. If the company does not, there are many private protection services that can give you the specific training you need. If you have or had an unstable relationship and fear that your significant other could abduct you, I urge you to learn all that you can about protecting yourself from this crime. This training is more in depth and specific than is needed for most people. It could fill a book on its own, so I won't be covering those specifics here. If you think you might need the info, I encourage you to find it at the library, book store, on the internet and from security experts like www.gdbinc.com.

> **The number one thing to remember if someone grabs you and tries to force you to go with them-- *DON'T GO!***

Even if you resist and end up getting hurt in the location where they first make contact with you, you are much more likely to get help there.

> If you go with them to the location of their choice, it is unlikely that anyone will come to your aid or even find you.

Your top priorities should be to convince the attacker that you are not an easy victim and to get away. If you yell "help" bystanders, unfortunately, are less likely to respond. Instead, let people know what is happening and what they can do. Yell as loudly as possible, "Hey!" (Most people will look to see if you are talking to them), "Get his description! He's trying to abduct me!" Whenever possible, make direct eye contact with a witness so they know you are talking to them.

Use whatever means necessary to get away and do it as soon as you are grabbed. The primary targets of any strike you may make should be his eyes, throat and (if he's feeling pain) the groin. Strikes are fine if they are helping you get free, but don't stay and fight him-- your primary goal is to get loose so you can run away.

Another alternative was suggested in the book "Defensive Living" in which Bo Brady suggests you act like you have fainted. By lying in a limp heap on the ground, you make yourself very hard to move and you have not posed a threat to the attacker that he might feel compelled to handle. Only you will be able to make the determination from the situation which alternative-- fight or faint-- would seem most prudent.

> Regardless of which tactics you use,
> DON'T EVER go with the abductor!

If he has a weapon and is willing to use it on you at the public abduction site, you can be sure he plans an even worse fate when you are in private.

If he tells you "Don't Yell" he is actually telling you that yelling could be to your advantage. He doesn't want you to yell because someone might hear you. When he tells you "come with me" he is in effect telling you that he can't do what he wants with you in the current location.

Never get into a car with a stranger is commonly preached to kids, but it is sound advice for you too. **If you are a realtor, or your job involves going from one place to another with a client, please heed this advice!**

Always take separate cars or if they don't have a car use a taxi. You can tell the client you have another meeting to go to "if time allows" or that your car broke down. That way, you leave yourself open to spend as much time as needed with the client, but you don't compromise your safety by getting into a car with someone you barely know.

Don't let convenience be more important than your safety. Several realtors have been assaulted or killed by people they have been working with and have met on more than one occasion. In some cases, the attacker had been a client for over a month and several home showings had been done. Don't let familiarity with the client compromise your safety. You have no way to know if the person is off his medication, high, drunk or about to have a psychotic break until it's too late.

> Don't drop your guard because you have met with the client a few times.

If someone chooses to do harm to you, it won't matter if you are the driver or the passenger. As the driver, you can control where the vehicle goes, but if he has a weapon and you ignore his demands, he may choose to hurt or kill you before you reach safety. <u>As a last resort</u>, if you are driving on a busy road and your passenger is threatening you with a weapon, be sure your seatbelt is on, reduce your speed to <u>less than</u> 30 miles per hour and crash his side of the car into something close to the road (parked car, telephone pole, etc.) Try to give him as little time to react as possible. People are likely to stop and offer aid at a single car auto accident and there is a good chance the police and an ambulance will be dispatched. If you are in a parking lot try running into as many parked cars as possible. It's guaranteed you will draw attention! Do your best to avoid pedestrians and people walking between cars.

About rape

A stranger without a plan does not commit most rapes. Most rapes are committed by someone the victim knows; a family member, neighbor, co-worker, boss, friend, clergyman, doctor, or even a client. Often, the victim of an acquaintance rape says, "I never imagined he would do that to me!"

Usually the rape is planned. The rapist selects the area or location and the victim before making his first move. It is not usually a "crime of opportunity" and many are elaborately planned down to the fine details. Many rapists are repeat offenders and with each attack they are learning what works and what doesn't.

Of course not all rapes are so planned. If a rapist finds himself presented with an ideal victim in a private setting, he may decide to "go for it" even though he may not have intended to rape someone that day.

Rape is a crime of power, not sex. The crime is not committed for the sex. A large number of rapists are married and live an otherwise normal life. It is not likely that you would be able to pick a rapist out of a crowd. The best way to keep yourself from falling prey to a rapist is to not look like a victim. Re-read the *do you look like a victim* section and put those tips into practice in your daily life. Trust your instincts and have a plan. Don't drop your guard or ignore your instincts just because it is someone you know.

When you open your mind to the possibility that it is possible for your attacker to be someone you know, you won't be blind or in denial about the warning signals.

Protecting Yourself From Violence During Home Visits by Chris Puls

Weapons- yes or no

Some people consider carrying a weapon. Some already do. I don't recommend that you take a weapon into a client's home. I feel this way for several major reasons.

If you have a gun, then all contacts and encounters with other people are "armed encounters."

> Just because you control the weapon when you go in, does not mean you will keep control of it if the situation takes a turn for the worse.

Once the other person knows you have the weapon, there is the possibility that he will take it away from you and use it on you. Keep this in mind if you choose to carry *any* type of weapon.

You are asking for trouble if you are not familiar with and proficient in the use of the weapon you choose. There are training courses for all types of weapons and I encourage you to learn everything you can and get many hours of practice before you rely on the weapon in a serious situation. Even the purchase of non-lethal sprays that are readily available in most areas should also include the purchase of a training course. Learning to defend yourself with a weapon is no different from learning any other skill that involves muscle memory, it takes a lot of practice until it becomes second nature. The use of a weapon should be as natural as using your hand if you plan to rely on a weapon for self defense.

Training courses will help you become fully familiar with the weapon of your choice but only practice will make it an effective option. The course should also cover the laws regarding the use of the weapon and "use of force" laws. These laws will be the determining factor used to judge you if you have used force to stop an assailant and ignorance of the law is not a defense. If you do not like the thought of going to prison for defending yourself I suggest you become very familiar with these laws. If you work in different states, you need to be familiar with the laws in all of the states you might work in. If you carry a gun, be sure a concealed-carry permit from one state is valid in the others and be sure any non-lethal options you may choose are legal.

Regardless of what you choose to carry, if you have not made up your mind, without a doubt, that you WILL use the weapon (to cause death should the need arise) you are likely to hesitate or miss your target. It also makes it much more likely that your weapon will be taken and used on you. If you cannot honestly say you could use serious force, including force that could cause death, don't carry a weapon.

It has been documented time and again that if the person with the weapon does not want to cause injury or death, they will hesitate, or miss the target.

One such case was a police officer that fired multiple shots at a drug crazed criminal while the criminal was charging the officer in a stairway (a very confined space with no cover). Not a single shot hit the criminal, even though the officer was proficient with the weapon at the target range and in a shooting simulator. She admitted that she didn't want to hurt the criminal even though the shooting would have been fully justified.

The criminal attacked the officer causing minor injuries (which could have been much worse) and then escaped. He was apprehended later by a different officer.

Another reason against taking a weapon into a client's home is kids. Kids are very investigative, especially of new things in their environments.

> Could you live with yourself if a child got into your bag, found your weapon and hurt or killed himself or a family member? How do you feel about going to prison?

If you think a weapon in a purse or briefcase will protect you, think again. Most attacks are a surprise. This means you don't have time to dig something out of your bag. If it's not in your hand or accessible within 2 seconds you probably won't have time to get your hands on it. There are many reasons that criminals have learned that using speed and surprise is to their advantage. It elicits an adrenalin dump in the victim, causes the victim to hesitate and prevents them from getting a weapon in their hand.

If you feel you absolutely must carry a weapon, I suggest that you choose one that is non-lethal. Pepper or chemical sprays, tazers and stun guns are possibilities. You still need to be very proficient in their use as well as have the proper mind set to use them. You take on the responsibility of keeping them out of the hands of children and being familiar with any laws that pertain to the carry or use of the weapon. They could still be used against you, but won't kill you.

Each weapon has positives attributes as well as drawbacks:

'Mace' or tear gas spray (also known as CS or CN spray)
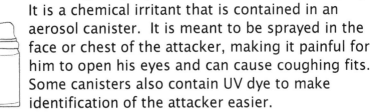
It is a chemical irritant that is contained in an aerosol canister. It is meant to be sprayed in the face or chest of the attacker, making it painful for him to open his eyes and can cause coughing fits. Some canisters also contain UV dye to make identification of the attacker easier.

Drawbacks:
- Does not work on all people
- Can take 3-30 seconds to take effect
- Aerosol has a limited 'shelf' life (replace canisters once a year)
- Has a limited range, some types more than others
- Sprays in a stream that can be hard to get onto your target
- Sprays in a "cone" shape are more affected by wind
- Can 'backfire' if sprayed into the wind
- Not legal in all cities or areas. Check with your local police department about purchase and possession.
- Could cause a person with asthma to die due to the constriction of airways

Benefits:
- You don't usually have to be within reach of the attacker
- Inexpensive
- Legal in many areas
- Easy to learn to use

Pepper Spray (also known as O.C. spray)

It is a derivative of a type of pepper plant. It is meant to be sprayed in the face of an attacker. It causes almost immediate swelling and temporary blindness as well as coughing and choking.

Generally sprays in a 'cone shaped' pattern that is easier to aim.

Drawbacks:
- Has a limited shelf life (replace each year)
- Not all brands are created equal or contain the same percentage of pepper. Look for canisters containing at least 1% O.C.
- Can backfire if sprayed into the wind
- Not legal in all cities or areas. Check with your local police.
- Can cause a person with asthma to die due to the constriction of airways

Benefits:
- You don't have to be within reach of the attacker
- Inexpensive
- Legal in many areas
- Easy to learn to use
- Fast acting

Note: I don't recommend leaving any canister in a hot car during the summer unless it is designed to withstand high temperatures. The heat can cause the aerosol to expand causing the canister to leak. Not a pleasant experience.

I do recommend that you attend a training class for any device or weapon you choose. Your local police department or gun shop should be able to put you in touch with the proper instructors.

Stun Gun
It is a compact box with two prongs at one end. An electrical charge is delivered when the trigger is pressed and the prongs contact a person.

Drawbacks:
- You have to be within reach of the attacker
- Batteries need to be kept charged
- Not legal to carry in all states/cities
- Thick clothing may reduce effectiveness
- Determined or drugged assailants may be able to attack during the charge or as soon as the charge is discontinued.

Benefits:
- sound alone may prevent an attack
- Easy to use

Tazers

Most look like a square shaped, plastic gun. When "fired" it sends out a barbed prong that attaches in the person's skin. A fine wire attaches the barb to the gun where the power source is located. As long as the trigger is pressed, the charge is delivered. The charge interrupts and overloads the electrical signals sent between the muscles and the brain.

Drawbacks:
- These are fairly new for public use and are not readily available
- Batteries have to be kept charged
- You have to be proficient with their use
- Not legal to be carried in all states/cities
- Determined or drugged assailants may be able to attack as soon as the charge is discontinued.
- May be mistaken for a gun
- Thick clothing may reduce effectiveness or cause failure
- Bulky and hard to conceal

Benefits:
- Can be very effective if conditions are right

For more information or to purchase these products, simply search the Internet or visit a gun shop. Some of the larger sporting goods stores also carry pepper and chemical sprays or mixes of both types.

Regardless of the weapon you might choose, it will only work if it is in your hand at the moment it is needed. It will not prevent a surprise attack and if it is in your purse you won't have time to get it out, remove the safety, aim and use it.

Rather than having a weapon that could be used by others against you-- learn self-defense.
This has many benefits, even if you never have to use it in real life. Knowing how to physically protect yourself is empowering.

> Physical self-defense knowledge gives you confidence that radiates, "I will not be a victim"

It is also great exercise and it cannot be turned against you in the way a weapon could. The drawback is the time and commitment involved.

For most styles, becoming proficient enough to use martial arts, to defend yourself in real time, takes years to master. If you don't want to devote that much time to it, I suggest you opt for a self-defense course. The key to making that work is practice.

You won't have the repertoire of a martial artist, but you will know a few key moves that, with repeated practice, can become very effective and second nature to you.

Other situations

There are other situations that are possible that neither you nor the client has control over, but that still pose a serious hazard or emergency situation.

Fire-
Would you know how to get out of that apartment building you are visiting for the first time if a fire broke out? Did you pay attention to where the stairwell was in relation to the client's door? Fire and the resulting smoke can spread more rapidly that you might imagine. You can't rely on the client to know where the stairs are located because he may always take the elevator.

Unless he has made a conscious effort to know how many doors are between his door and the stairs, he may not be able to find them in a hall full of smoke. If a fire breaks out or you smell smoke, your only concern should be getting you and the client(s) out of the building as fast as possible.

Don't try to fight the fire, don't try to call 911 from inside the home, just get out! You can call from a neighbor's phone or from the cell phone you should have with you.

If exit through a door is not an option, go through a window. If the window is too high, use a light colored towel or sheet to signal fire fighters to your window. Most fire ladders won't be able to reach an exterior window that is higher than the 7th floor.

If trapped, cover vents and put a wet towel or sheet at the bottom of any door exposed to the area where the fire is located. This will help minimize the amount of smoke that can get into the room. Open or break an outside window to get fresh air to breathe. Soak blankets you can wrap around you and soak your clothes to help stay cool and prevent your clothes from catching on fire if you need to run through small flames for a short distance to get to a stairwell. Stay low to get under smoke. Most victims of house fires are killed by the smoke before the fire ever reaches them.

There are products on the market that will give you a few minutes of clean oxygen to breathe so you can get through smoke to an exit. A fire escape hood and fire blanket as well as other safety products are available at AlwaysBePrepared.com

Medical Emergency-
What would you do if the client had a heart attack? What if they were choking? What if they fell and broke a bone? What if one of these things happened to you while you were with the client?

> I highly recommend that everyone take a Red Cross First Aid course and stay current with that knowledge though refresher courses. You could literally have the client's life in your hands; you should take it upon yourself to learn what to do.

Because this is not a medical manual, I will not go into details about how to handle specific medical emergencies. The Red Cross does a great job of teaching people to save lives. They also have a few nice books on the subject that you can refer to on occasion to refresh your memory. If it has been awhile since you

have taken a course (or if you have never taken a course) please attend one.
Don't wait till you are faced with an emergency and find yourself wishing you had learned what to do.

Unsafe or unsanitary living conditions-
Depending on your profession, you may be more or less likely to come across this hazard. Some examples would be:

- The boards on the porch or in the house are rotten and loose.
- There are no working toilets and the existing ones are over flowing.
- There is a roach, mouse or rat infestation.
- The client has too many pets to care for them properly.
- The client's belongings are stacked in piles so high they could fall on you and no floor is visible.

As a police officer, I saw all of the above conditions and more. The conditions that some people live in are shocking.

These are all situations where you have to decide if you are comfortable and capable of doing your job under those conditions. If it is your job to handle those types of conditions, then you already expect the worst when you get an appointment. You should be better equipped, both mentally and physically (with proper equipment), to handle the situation. For the rest of us, it is more likely that we will be telling the client that we are not going to be able to help them. As I mentioned earlier in the scenarios section, there may be several different agencies you could contact to help the client if they are open to that help.

Insurance

We live in a very litigious society. People are suing other people for anything and everything. If you are not covered by insurance through your company or if you are self-employed, you may need to consider getting insurance. In some cases, insurance provided by the company is very minimal and you may need additional coverage to put your mind at ease and protect your personal assets in the event of a claim.

The type of policy you get would depend upon the job you do and the potential hazards you face. If you are a self employed organizer of clutter, you will want to at least get liability insurance to cover anything you might break or accidentally sort into the trash while doing your job. The National Association of Professional Organizers has a policy available to the organizers that are paid members. If your profession has a trade association, check with that organization to see if insurance is available. If not, check with any insurance agent to inquire about possibilities for coverage. As with home, life and auto insurance, rates and coverage vary so shop around.

If you are a health care provider, you may need to have some form of "malpractice" coverage. I urge you to talk with your employer to find out just how much coverage is provided for you. If you feel it is not enough, talk to your insurance provider or employer about how you can get enough coverage to put your mind at ease.

Protecting Yourself From Violence During Home Visits by Chris Puls

Places to get more info

There have been many books written about physical self-defense as well as some about preparing you for danger though mental exercises. I encourage you to explore these books. Simply do a search on the Internet or at your local library or bookstore for topics like self defense, safety or survival signals to find them.

I have listed a few of my favorites on the resources page. I also encourage you to look for classes that teach (and let you practice) some of the simple and easy to use physical defense moves through programs such as IMPACT, Model Mugging or similar courses. Check with fitness centers, YMCA/YWCA, rape crisis centers or your local karate dojos to see if self defense classes for women are offered.

Regardless of where you find a class, be sure that you will have some male "assailants" to practice with so that you can get accustomed to feeling their strength and height differences.

Perhaps other women in your profession or your friends would be interested in taking the class(es) with you and then getting together for practice sessions to keep everyone's skills sharp.

If you are willing to devote a year or (in most cases) many more, then Martial Arts training can be very empowering. It can teach you some great defensive moves and effective counter attacks. You'll learn balance, confident body language and a proper mindset. There are so many different styles to choose from, you are likely to find one that suits you. There are over 1900 arts/styles listed on the Martial Arts of the World website!

In some martial arts styles, when you reach black belt, you then go back to a white belt (the beginner level). This is because you have gained enough knowledge to realize just how much there is to still be learned.
Keep in mind that becoming proficient enough to use these motor skills in real life doesn't happen over night and in the case of the more difficult techniques, could take many years to perfect.

Training in a class setting if very different from real life where stress, fear and adrenalin can affect your motor skills and your thinking. Regardless of whether you choose to learn many different techniques or just a few, continued practice is the key to being able to use them effectively.

Aftermath

The following information is provided so that you will understand what you are going through (or went though) if you have been the victim of an attack in the past. It will also help you know what to expect if you become a victim in the future and possibly give you motivation to learn all that  you can so you can avoid these effects.

> I have presented the effects to show why it is so critical to avoid becoming a victim. Avoiding the following effects of trauma is much easier than dealing with them after an attack.

Many times, victims think they are alone or unique in their symptoms and that the symptoms will eventually go away. It is true that with enough time, most will go away, but some never will and you can recover much more quickly with the help of a qualified professional.

The list below will also help friends, family and co-workers better understand some of the victim's reactions.

I provide the following information in case you are confronted with a determined attacker that won't let you escape a situation or you become the victim of a crime you have no control over, such as a group hostage situation or surprise attack. In which case, you will very likely go through some or all of the changes below.

These are normal and to be expected. I urge you to talk with an expert that can help you sort through the feelings and fears as soon as possible after the trauma.

Preparation and safety will go a long way to keeping you out of dangerous situations and keeping you from being a victim. Sadly, it is not always enough. Remember, you could only use the information and skills you had at that time. You cannot second guess yourself or berate yourself for not handling it better.

> Crime is not the victim's fault.

Effects of traumatic stress from a violent encounter:
- Shock and numbness may be the first effects
- Feeling angry and taking it out on those you love.
- Desire for revenge or vengeance.
- Recurring bad dreams or replaying the event in your mind repeatedly is common.
- Feeling afraid that your attacker will find you or that another attack will occur if you go back to work.
- Pervasive fear and/or anxiety.
- Self destructive or impulsive behaviors.
- Feeling ashamed of what has happened to you.
- Feeling unclean, even after bathing. These feelings may cause you to behave in ways you normally would not.
- Being overprotective of your own and your family's safety.
- Not being able to sleep or you may have terrible nightmares.

- Over working yourself to keep from thinking about the trauma.
- Changes in eating habits.
- Feeling helpless or ineffective because it seems you have lost control of your life.
- Not wanting to be left alone or you may not want human contact.
- You may not be able to resume your normal sexual relationships.
- Trouble concentrating and making decisions.
- Crying uncontrollably or feeling like you have no emotions.
- Hyper sensitive to touch or sudden noises.
- Depression

Immediate intervention can help you get on the road to recovery much faster. If you have been a victim, even if it was not recently and you are experiencing any of the above effects, I urge to talk to a professional about them.

What to do after an attack: If you are the victim of an attack or attempted attack, there are several things you should do.

1- **Always notify the police.** Even if you don't want to file charges against your attacker or you don't know who they are, you should notify the police and make a report so that they are aware of the assailant's actions. If he did it to you, he may have done it to someone else or try it again with another person. You may hold a small piece of information that is part of a larger puzzle. As a victim of certain types of attacks, you may feel more comfortable speaking with a female officer. If that is the case, just ask. The male officers understand and won't be offended.

2- <u>Don't change your clothes or take a shower.</u> Your skin can hold fingerprints and your clothes could have gun shot residue, fibers, hairs or fluids from the attacker. In the case of a sexual assault, showering can erase critical evidence. If you change your mind and decide to file charges later, it will be much more difficult without that critical evidence.

3- <u>Call someone that can be supportive.</u> In the event of a traumatic incident, it is helpful to have a friend, spouse or family member by your side. Also contact a rape crisis clinic.

They can provide you with a victim's advocate that can help you through the medical and legal process as well as be a great support and confidant. Most large cities have rape crisis counselors as well as hotlines that can put you in touch with an advocate in your area.

If you cannot find a center listed in your phone book the police and hospitals should have the contact numbers. You could also contact the National Center for the Victims of Crime: www.ncvc.org (800) FYI-CALL

Family members may need to speak to a counselor to help them cope with their own feelings and the things that are affecting the victim. Many marriages end because one or both people are not able to understand or cope with the aftermath.

4- If possible, <u>write down the following information while waiting for police to arrive</u>: (have any witnesses do the same)

Vehicle Identification
- Color or colors of vehicle
- Make/Model (Honda, Chevy, Toyota, etc.)
- Type (van, four door, pick up truck, etc.)
- Approximate age of vehicle (older model, newer model, etc.)
- License Plate number and state of issuance
- Window Tint, damage/dents, rust, bumper or window stickers or anything else that may be used to identify the vehicle.

Driver/Suspect Identification
- Race/Nationality (White, Black, Hispanic, etc.)
- Gender
- Hair (Color, Length, mustache, beard, balding, receding hairline, etc.)
- Height
- Weight
- Clothes (color/style of shirt, jacket, hat, glasses)
- Scars/Tattoos or injuries
- Speech peculiarities/accent
- Other passengers or partners
- Description of accomplices

5- Try to keep people out of the crime scene prior to the arrival of the police.

6- If the attacker runs away, watch where he goes so that a police dog can be used to follow him. If possible, keep people out of the path he took because many police dogs are trained to follow the freshest scent.

7- Anything the attacker touched should be preserved as evidence for the police to collect. This means that, unless it will be destroyed, you should not touch or move it. Be sure to point out these items to the police.

8- Preserve your clothes in a paper bag (not plastic) if they are needed for evidence.

9- Keep telling yourself to take deep slow breaths. They will help calm you down as much as possible.

10- Know that you will get through this. You will survive. Use positive thoughts and do your best to avoid negative thoughts or actions. Try to surround yourself with positive and supportive people.

My wish to you

I hope that you have been brave enough to read all of the pages in this book. I know thinking about your safety can be a very scary matter and being aware of the dangers can make them seem more real.

> It's OK to feel more apprehension. As you learn to handle and control those new feelings you can learn to use them to your advantage.

As you learn the ways to handle various scary situations, the apprehension will go away. You will be less likely to freeze in a difficult or dangerous situation. Remember to use the power of positive thinking. You can survive, you do have the knowledge to overcome danger and you will fight for <u>you</u> to protect your family from grief.

Raise your SAT score-
- **S**tay aware
- **A**ct on your warning signals
- **T**rust your instincts

If you haven't done so already, I suggest you reassess your SAT score by answering the questions at the beginning of the book. Discussion of the answers follows this section.

Even if you don't feel that you have a fighting bone in your body and even if you aren't currently using confident body language; it doesn't mean you can't develop the habits and have it work for you!

At one conference I had a woman stand up that was very petit. She said "I don't look like you. I'm not big and tall and strong." She made it sound like I am a pro wrestler or something <grin>

But I'm of average height, I weigh... more than I should, but what makes me look more imposing is my confidence. My body language says I mean business.

- By developing some possible plans for situations you think you could encounter
- Developing your instincts by learning about possible situations and ploys
- Turning your new skills into habits and
- Developing and strengthening the mental switch between reaction brain and thinking brain...

You WILL be much safer.

It all depends on your willingness to learn and practice. You are the only one you can count on for your protection.

I've given you a lot of information. As you read and re-read this book, pick out the things that you can incorporate into your routine easily and practice those things until they become habit.

Once you have developed those habits, go back through and pick out things that are a little more difficult to implement and make those into habits.

> By using this method, you can teach yourself many new behaviors and positive habits without getting overwhelmed. It will make you feel good to take an active roll in your safety.

You won't be relying on luck, the odds or someone else to keep you safe. It can give you a sense of security you may have never had before.

My wish is that you never have the occasion to use any of the defensive maneuvers in this book, but if the occasion arises, that you are able to put this information to good use and that it helps you stay safe.

> Success in personal protection is not winning a fight, but instead-- avoiding it.

The ultimate success is when nothing happens! If that's not possible, consider this philosophy:

If you can't prevent it, avoid it.
If you can't avoid it, defuse it.
If you can't defuse it, escape.
If you can't escape, you may have to fight.
If you have to fight, fight for your loved ones.

If you are willing to learn how to project confidence, it doesn't matter what size you are or even how you feel inside. People will see you as a person to be noticed and respected; and the predators won't give you a second look.

If you have found this book to be helpful or have a success story to share I would love to know. Please email them to **SafeHomeVisits@hotmail.com** If I can use your comments and/or story on my website or brochures, please let me know that as well.

Peace,
Chris Puls

Protecting Yourself From Violence During Home Visits by Chris Puls

Some additional notes about the S.A.T. assessment

#1- D. is the preferred choice

#2- C. is the preferred choice

#3- Any of the choices could be possible depending on the level of warning your intuition is sending you.

#4- A. and B. could cause you to look fearful and increase your chances of being selected as a target. So C. would be the preferred choice

#5- C. is the correct choice

#6- If you chose A. you need to re-read the section on denial. B. is not suggested because it puts the items into the person's hands where they could decide to use it on you. C. is the preferred choice

#7- A. - making a series of turns- would only be advisable if you were in an area with lots of other people such as a business complex or shopping area and you knew where you were going. B. Varying your speed, such as slowing down well below the speed of most others cars, to see if the following person will pass is a possibility if there is a way for him to get by you. C. is also a possibility, just be sure you don't park in such a way that allows him to block you in. D. would be the suggested choice

#8- B. is not recommended because you don't want to dismiss your feelings. D. would be the preferred choice

#9- D. would be the preferred choice

#10- This situation could indicate someone that doesn't handle rejection well or that has a controlling personality. Either way, staying around to debate with him (B.) only delays the inevitable. If you notice, he has used a "compelling statement" (one of the warning signals) to try to guilt you into staying. If you choose A. and give in, he could see that as a signal that you can be dominated and controlled. C. is the preferred choice.

If he were to continue to call or see you in person and try to talk to you, notify the police. It could be the start of stalking behavior.

#11- Joke or no joke, this is NOT acceptable behavior and it is not funny. Even though he makes you think he was joking, it could have been a test of your reaction. A. is not a recommended choice. B. is also not recommended because you are admitting that you were very uncomfortable which may be exactly what he wants. Therefore, C. would be the preferred choice. Remain calm and in control, tell him to "Move. Now." Then walk out.

#12- You should not have to tolerate being made uncomfortable by a client's actions or words. If you give in and move he could see it as yielding behavior and a higher chance that you can be manipulated or controlled. C. is the preferred choice because it keeps you in control. If the person meant no harm by it, it is not offensive to request that he "please move over."

#13- Your reaction to this could depend on the signals your intuition is sending you or you could make the choice to leave simply because you are well out numbered. Warning signals to watch for from the group would include but not be limited to: extended staring or catching them all looking at you, crude comments, improper smiles that suggest ill intent or crude thoughts and any attempt to get behind you or to touch you.

#14- This is another situation in which your instincts will be your guide. Congratulate yourself for noticing the stance and choose to raise your awareness a notch if you feel the behaviors or situation warrants it. Having the person sit is a good way to attempt to diffuse the potential for trouble in this situation.

#15- The reaction to this could depend on how obvious the person is about following you and the amount of hostility you get from him. If you sense any hostility or the person is making no attempt to hide the fact that he is following you, then he's trying to cause fear. Remain calm and call the police. Keep the dispatcher on the phone until a patrol car arrives. If he is attempting to hide the fact that he is following you and doesn't know you have seen him, then choice A. or B. could be an option. Be ready to switch to C. if you sense danger. Blowing the horn of your car non-stop is another way to attract attention to the situation. Be sure your car doors are locked and don't get out until he is gone or police arrive.

Congratulations on raising your S.A.T. score. Continue to look for ways you can get it even higher because you are worth it!

Recommended books and videos

The Gift of Fear by Gavin de Becker
ISBN: 0440226198

Be Alert, Be Aware, Have a Plan: The Complete Guide to Personal Security by Neal Rawls, Sue Kovach
ISBN: 1585745774

Defensive Living by Bo Hardy
ISBN: 0963323792

How to Live Safely in a Dangerous World by Loren Christensen
ISBN: 0918751454

Fierce and Female Practical Rape Defense Tactics for Every Woman - Video Set by Melissa Soalt
Available from www.Paladin-Press.com
ISBN: 1581601263

Notes:
1. D.G. Sarvadi, Environmental Law Handbook, Government Institute, 1993
2. November 25, 1996, Page 2B, Miami Herald,
3. Thursday, October 18, 2001 Cincinnati Enquirer
4. Dodge City Daily Globe Feb 2000
5. November 7, 2003 Akron Beacon-Journal
6. Safetyoptions.com/Community%20Workers
7. FBI Law Enforcement Bulletin- Realtor-Police Partnership for Safety by Karl Leonard
8. Cincinnati Enquirer Feb 2006
9. U.S. Department of Labor; Bureau of Labor Statistics

ISBN 1412092-2

9 781412 092920

Made in the USA
Lexington, KY
24 June 2011